# COMMON CORE MATHEMATICS

## A Story of Functions

## Algebra I, Module 5: A Synthesis of Modeling with Equations and Functions

*consider the source*

## JOSSEY-BASS™

A Wiley Brand

Cover design by Chris Clary

Published by Jossey-Bass
A Wiley Brand
One Montgomery Street, Suite 1200, San Francisco, CA 94104-4594—www.josseybass.com

ISBN: 978-1-118-81128-3

Printed in the United States of America
FIRST EDITION
*PB Printing*      10  9  8  7  6  5  4  3  2  1

# WELCOME

Dear Teacher,

Thank you for your interest in Common Core's curriculum in mathematics. Common Core is a non-profit organization based in Washington, DC dedicated to helping K-12 public schoolteachers use the power of high-quality content to improve instruction.[1] We are led by a board of master teachers, scholars, and current and former school, district, and state education leaders. Common Core has responded to the Common Core State Standards' (CCSS) call for "content-rich curriculum"[2] by creating new, CCSS-based curriculum materials in mathematics, English Language Arts, history, and (soon) the arts. All of our materials are written by teachers who are among the nation's foremost experts on the new standards.

In 2012 Common Core won three contracts from the New York State Education Department to create a PreKindergarten–12th grade mathematics curriculum for the teachers of that state, and to conduct associated professional development. The book you hold contains a portion of that work. In order to respond to demand in New York and elsewhere, modules of the curriculum will continue to be published, on a rolling basis, as they are completed. This curriculum is based on New York's version of the CCSS (the CCLS, or Common Core Learning Standards). Common Core will be releasing an enhanced version of the curriculum this summer on our website, commoncore.org. That version also will be published by Jossey-Bass, a Wiley brand.

Common Core's curriculum materials are not merely aligned to the new standards, they take the CCSS as their very foundation. Our work in math takes its shape from the expectations embedded in the new standards—including the instructional shifts and mathematical progressions, and the new expectations for student fluency, deep conceptual understanding, and application to real-life context. Similarly, our ELA and history curricula are deeply informed by the CCSS's new emphasis on close reading, increased use of informational text, and evidence-based writing.

Our curriculum is distinguished not only by its adherence to the CCSS. The math curriculum is based on a theory of teaching math that is proven to work. That theory posits that mathematical knowledge is most coherently and

---

1. Despite the coincidence of name, Common Core and the Common Core State Standards are not affiliated. Common Core was established in 2007, prior to the start of the Common Core State Standards Initiative, which was led by the National Governors Association and the Council for Chief State School Officers.

2. *Common Core State Standards for English Language Arts & Literacy in History/Social Studies, Science, and Technical Subjects* (Washington, DC: Common Core State Standards Initiative), 6.

effectively conveyed when it is taught in a sequence that follows the "story" of mathematics itself. This is why we call the elementary portion of this curriculum "A Story of Units," to be followed by "A Story of Ratios" in middle school, and "A Story of Functions" in high school. Mathematical concepts flow logically, from one to the next, in this curriculum. The sequencing has been joined with methods of instruction that have been proven to work, in this nation and abroad. These methods drive student understanding beyond process, to deep mastery of mathematical concepts. The goal of the curriculum is to produce students who are not merely literate, but fluent, in mathematics.

It is important to note that, as extensive as these curriculum materials are, they are not meant to be prescriptive. Rather, they are intended to provide a basis for teachers to hone their own craft through study, collaboration, training, and the application of their own expertise as professionals. At Common Core we believe deeply in the ability of teachers and in their central and irreplaceable role in shaping the classroom experience. We strive only to support and facilitate their important work.

The teachers and scholars who wrote these materials are listed beginning on the next page. Their deep knowledge of mathematics, of the CCSS, and of what works in classrooms defined this work in every respect. I would like to thank Louisiana State University professor of mathematics Scott Baldridge for the intellectual leadership he provides to this project. Teacher and trainer Jill Diniz, who is the lead writer for grades 6–12, has brought extraordinary intelligence and judgment to this work. Jill's ability to thrive in situations in which others would be lucky just to persevere, is uncommon.

Finally, this work owes a debt to project director Nell McAnelly that is so deep I'm confident it never can be repaid. Nell, who leads LSU's Gordon A. Cain Center for STEM Literacy, oversees all aspects of our work for NYSED. She has spent days, nights, weekends, and many cancelled vacations toiling in her efforts to make it possible for this talented group of teacher-writers to produce their best work against impossible deadlines. I'm confident that in the years to come Scott, Robin, and Nell will be among those who will deserve to be credited with putting math instruction in our nation back on track.

Thank you for taking an interest in our work. Please join us at www.commoncore.org.

Lynne Munson
President and Executive Director
Common Core
Washington, DC
October 25, 2013

## Common Core's 6-12 Math Staff

Scott Baldridge, Lead Mathematician and Writer
Robin Ramos, Lead Writer, PreKindergarten–5
Ben McCarty, Mathematician

Nell McAnelly, Project Director
Tiah Alphonso, Associate Director
Jennifer Loftin, Associate Director
Catriona Anderson, Curriculum Manager,
   PreKindergarten–5
Jill Diniz, Lead Writer, 9-11 and Curriculum
   Manager

### Sixth Grade

Erika Silva, Lead
Debby Grawn
Glenn Gebhard
Krysta Gibbs

### Sixth and Seventh Grade

Anne Netter, Lead
Beau Bailey
Saki Milton
Hester Sutton
David Wright
Korinna Sanchez

### Seventh Grade

Julie Wortmann, Lead
Joanne Choi
Lori Fanning
Bonnie Hart

### Eighth Grade

Stefanie Hassan, Lead
Winnie Gilbert
Sunil Koswatta, Mathematician

### Ninth Grade

Miki Alkire
Chris Bejar
Carlos Carrera
Melvin Damaolao
Joe Ferrantelli
Jenny Kim
Athena Leonardo

Rob Michelin
Noam Pillischer
Alex Sczesnak

### Tenth Grade

Pia Mohsen, Lead
Bonnie Bergstresser
Ellen Fort
Terrie Poehl

### Ninth, Tenth, and Eleventh Grade

Kevin Bluount
Wendy DenBesten
Abe Frankel
Thomas Gaffey
Kay Gleenblatt
Sheri Goings
Pam Goodner
Selena Oswalt
William Rorison
Chris Murcko
Surinder Sandhu
Pam Walker
Darrick Wood

### Statistics

Henry Kranendonk, Lead
Michael Allwood
Gail Burrill
Beth Chance
Brian Kotz
Kathy Kritz
Patrick Hopsfensperger
Jerry Moren
Shannon Vinson

### Document Management Team

Kristen Zimmerman

### Advisors

Richard Askey
Roger Howe
James Madden
Roxy Peck
James Tanton

Table of Contents[1]

# A Synthesis of Modeling with Equations and Functions

*Topics A and B (assessment 2 days, return 4 days, remediation or further applications 5 days)*

---

[1] Each lesson is one day and one day is considered a 45 minute period.

# Algebra I • Module 5

# A Synthesis of Modeling with Equations and Functions

## OVERVIEW

In Grade 8, students use functions for the first time to construct a function to model a linear relationship between two quantities (**8.F.4**) and to describe qualitatively the functional relationship between two quantities by analyzing a graph (**8.F.5**). In the first four modules of Grade 9, students learn to create and apply linear, quadratic, and exponential functions, in addition to square and cube root functions (**F-IF.C.7**). In Module 5, they synthesize what they have learned during the year by selecting the correct function type in a series of modeling problems without the benefit of a module or lesson title that includes function type to guide them in their choices. This supports the CCSS requirement that students use the modeling cycle, in the beginning of which they must formulate a strategy. Skills and knowledge from the previous modules will support the requirements of this module, including writing, rewriting, comparing, and graphing functions (**F-IF.C.7**, **F-IF.C.8**, **F-IF.C.9**) and interpretation of the parameters of an equation (**F-LE.B.5**). They also draw on their study of statistics in Module 2, using graphs and functions to model a context presented with data and/or tables of values (**S-ID.B.6**). In this module, we use the modeling cycle (see page 72 of the CCSS) as the organizing structure, rather than function type.

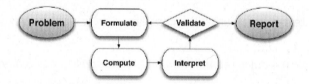

Topic A focuses on the skills inherent in the modeling process: representing graphs, data sets, or verbal descriptions using explicit expressions (**F-BF.A.1a**) when presented in graphic form in Lesson 1, as data in Lesson 2, or as a verbal description of a contextual situation in Lesson 3. They recognize the function type associated with the problem (**F-LE.A.1b**, **F-LE.A.1c**) and match to or create 1- and 2-variable equations (**A-CED.A.1**, **A-CED.2**) to model a context presented graphically, as a data set, or as a description (**F-LE.A.2**). Function types include linear, quadratic, exponential, square root, cube root, absolute value, and other piecewise functions. Students interpret features of a graph in order to write an equation that can be used to model it and the function (**F-IF.B.4**, **F-BF.A.1**) and relate the domain to both representations (**F-IF.B.5**). This topic focuses on the skills needed to complete the modeling cycle and sometimes uses purely mathematical models, sometimes real-world contexts.

Tables, graphs, and equations all represent models. We use terms such as "symbolic" or "analytic" to refer specifically to the equation form of a function model; "descriptive model" refers to a model that seeks to describe or summarize phenomena, such as a graph. In Topic B, students expand on their work in Topic A to complete the modeling cycle for a real-world contextual problem presented as a graph, a data set, or a verbal

description. For each, they *formulate* a function model, perform *computations* related to solving the problem, *interpret* the problem and the model, and then, through iterations of revising their models as needed, *validate*, and *report* their results.

Students choose and define the quantities of the problem (**N-Q.A.2**) and the appropriate level of precision for the context (**N-Q.A.3**). They create 1- and 2-variable equations (**A-CED.A.1**, **A-CED.A.2**) to model the context when presented as a graph, as data and as a verbal description. They can distinguish between situations that represent a linear (**F-LE.A.1b**), quadratic, or exponential (**F-LE.A.1c**) relationship. For data, they look for first differences to be constant for linear, second differences to be constant for quadratic, and a common ratio for exponential. When there are clear patterns in the data, students will recognize when the pattern represents a linear (arithmetic) or exponential (geometric) sequence (**F-BF.A.1a**, **F-LE.A.2**). For graphic presentations, they interpret the key features of the graph, and for both data sets and verbal descriptions they sketch a graph to show the key features (**F-IF.B.4**). They calculate and interpret the average rate of change over an interval, estimating when using the graph (**F-IF.B.6**), and relate the domain of the function to its graph and to its context (**F-IF.B.5**).

# Focus Standards

## Reason quantitatively and use units to solve problems.

**N-Q.A.2**[2]     Define appropriate quantities for the purpose of descriptive modeling.

**N-Q.A.3**     Choose a level of accuracy appropriate to limitations on measurement when reporting quantities.

## Create equations that describe numbers or relationships.

**A-CED.A.1**[3]    Create equations and inequalities in one variable and use them to solve problems. *Include equations arising from linear and quadratic functions, and simple rational and exponential functions.*★

**A-CED.A.2**    Create equations in two or more variables to represent relationships between quantities; graph equations on coordinate axes with labels and scales.★

## Interpret functions that arise in applications in terms of the context.

**F-IF.B.4**     For a function that models a relationship between two quantities, interpret key features of graphs and tables in terms of the quantities, and sketch graphs showing key features given a verbal description of the relationship. *Key features include: intercepts; intervals where the function is increasing, decreasing, positive, or negative; relative maximums and minimums; symmetries; end behavior; and periodicity.*★[4]

---

[2] This standard will be assessed in Algebra I by ensuring that some modeling tasks (involving Algebra I content or securely held content from Grades 6–8) require the student to create a quantity of interest in the situation being described.

[3] In Algebra I, tasks are limited to linear, quadratic, or exponential equations with integer exponents.

[4] Note: Tasks have a real-world context. In Algebra I, tasks are limited to linear, quadratic, square root, cube root, piecewise-defined (including step and absolute value functions), and exponential functions with domains in the integers.

---

**F-IF.B.5**  Relate the domain of a function to its graph and, where applicable, to the quantitative relationship it describes. *For example, if the function h(n) gives the number of person-hours it takes to assemble n engines in a factory, then the positive integers would be an appropriate domain for the function.*★

**F-IF.B.6**  Calculate and interpret the average rate of change of a function (presented symbolically or as a table) over a specified interval. Estimate the rate of change from a graph.★[5]

## Build a function that models a relationship between two quantities.

**F-BF.A.1**[6]  Write a function that describes a relationship between two quantities.★

    a.  Determine an explicit expression, a recursive process, or steps for calculation from a context.

## Construct and compare linear, quadratic, and exponential models and solve problems.

**F-LE.A.1**  Distinguish between situations that can be modeled with linear functions and with exponential functions.★

    b.  Recognize situations in which one quantity changes at a constant rate per unit interval relative to another.

    c.  Recognize situations in which a quantity grows or decays by a constant percent rate per unit interval relative to another.

**F-LE.A.2**[7]  Construct linear and exponential functions, including arithmetic and geometric sequences, given a graph, a description of a relationship, or two input-output pairs (include reading these from a table).★

# Foundational Standards

## Use functions to model relationships between quantities.

**8.F.B.4**  Construct a function to model a linear relationship between two quantities. Determine the rate of change and initial value of the function from a description of a relationship or from two (*x, y*) values, including reading these from a table or from a graph. Interpret the rate of change and initial value of a linear function in terms of the situation it models, and in terms of its graph or a table of values.

**8.F.B.5**  Describe qualitatively the functional relationship between two quantities by analyzing a graph (e.g., where the function is increasing or decreasing, linear or nonlinear). Sketch a graph that exhibits the qualitative features of a function that has been described verbally.

---

[5] Note: Tasks have a real-world context. In Algebra I, tasks are limited to linear, quadratic, square root, cube root, piecewise-defined (including step functions and absolute value functions), and exponential functions with domains in the integers.

[6] Tasks have a real-world context. In Algebra I, tasks are limited to linear functions, quadratic functions, and exponential functions with domains in the integers.

[7] In Algebra I, tasks are limited to constructing linear and exponential functions in simple context (not multi-step).

---

Module 5:    A Synthesis of Modeling with Equations and Functions
Date:      10/4/13

## Analyze functions using different representations.

**F-IF.C.7**  Graph functions expressed symbolically and show key features of the graph, by hand in simple cases and using technology for more complicated cases.[★]

    a.  Graph linear and quadratic functions and show intercepts, maxima, and minima.

    b.  Graph square root, cube root, and piecewise-defined functions, including step functions and absolute value functions.

**F-IF.C.8**  Write a function defined by an expression in different but equivalent forms to reveal and explain different properties of the function.

    a.  Use the process of factoring and completing the square in a quadratic function to show zeros, extreme values, and symmetry of the graph, and interpret these in terms of a context.

**F-IF.C.9**[8]  Compare properties of two functions each represented in a different way (algebraically, graphically, numerically in tables, or by verbal descriptions). *For example, given a graph of one quadratic function and an algebraic expression for another, say which has the larger maximum.*

## Interpret expressions for functions in terms of the situation they model.

**F-LE.B.5**[9]  Interpret the parameters in a linear or exponential function in terms of a context.[★]

## Summarize, represent, and interpret data on two categorical and quantitative variables.

**S-ID.B.6**  Represent data on two quantitative variables on a scatter plot, and describe how the variables are related.[★]

    a.  Fit a function to the data; use functions fitted to data to solve problems in the context of the data. *Use given functions or choose a function suggested by the context. Emphasize linear, quadratic, and exponential models.*[10]

    b.  Informally assess the fit of a function by plotting and analyzing residuals.

# Focus Standards for Mathematical Practice

**MP.1**  **Make sense of problems and persevere in solving them.**  Mathematically proficient students start by explaining to themselves the meaning of a problem and looking for entry points to its solution.  They analyze givens, constraints, relationships, and goals.  In Module 5, students make sense of the problem by analyzing the critical components of the problem, presented as a verbal description, a data set, or a graph and persevere in writing the appropriate function that describes the relationship between two quantities.  Then, they interpret the function in the context.

---

[8] In Algebra I, tasks are limited to linear functions, quadratic functions, square root functions, cube root functions, piecewise-defined functions (including step functions and absolute value functions), and exponential functions with domains in the integers.

[9] Tasks have a real-world context.  In Algebra I, exponential functions are limited to those with domains in the integers.

[10] Tasks have a real-world context.  In Algebra I, exponential functions are limited to those with domains in the integers.

---

**MP.2**    **Reason abstractly and quantitatively.**  Mathematically proficient students make sense of quantities and their relationships in problem situations.  This module alternates between algebraic manipulation of expressions and equations and interpreting the quantities in the relationship in terms of the context.  In Topic A, students develop fluency in recognizing and identifying key features of the three primary function types studied in Grade 9, as well as manipulating expressions to highlight those features.  Topic B builds on these skills so that when students are given a verbal description of a situation that can be described by a function they *decontextualize it and apply the skills they learned in Topic A in order to further analyze the situation.*  Then, they *contextualize their work* so they can compare, interpret, and make predictions and claims.  In the assessment, students are frequently asked to explain their solutions so that teachers have a clear understanding of the reasoning behind their results.

**MP.4**    **Model with mathematics.**  Mathematically proficient students can apply the mathematics they know to solve problems arising in everyday life, society, and the workplace.  In this module, students create a function from a contextual situation described verbally, create a graph of their function, interpret key features of both the function and the graph in the terms of the context, and answer questions related to the function and its graph.  They also create a function from a data set based on a contextual situation.  In Topic B, students use the full modeling cycle with functions presented mathematically or in a context, including linear, quadratic, and exponential.  They explain their mathematical thinking in writing and/or by using appropriate tools, such as graph paper, graphing calculator, or computer software.

**MP.5**    **Use appropriate tools strategically.**  Mathematically proficient students consider the available tools when solving a mathematical problem.  These tools might include pencil and paper, concrete models, a ruler, a protractor, a calculator, a spreadsheet, a computer algebra system, a statistical package, or dynamic geometry software.  Proficient students are sufficiently familiar with tools appropriate for their grade or course to make sound decisions about when each of these tools might be helpful, recognizing both the insight to be gained and their limitations.  Throughout the entire module students must decide whether or not to use a tool to help find solutions.  They must graph functions that are sometimes difficult to sketch (e.g., cube root and square root) and sometimes are required to perform procedures that can be tedious, and sometimes distract from the mathematical thinking, when performed without technology (e.g., completing the square with non-integer coefficients).  In these cases, students must decide whether to use a tool to help with the calculation or graph so they can better analyze the model.  Students should have access to a graphing calculator for use on the module assessment.

**MP.6**    **Attend to precision.**  Mathematically proficient students try to communicate precisely to others.  They state the meaning of the symbols they choose, including using the equal sign consistently and appropriately.  They are careful about specifying units of measure and labeling axes to clarify the correspondence with quantities in a problem.  When calculating and reporting quantities in all topics of Module 5 students must choose the appropriate units and use the appropriate level of precision based on the information as it is presented.  When graphing they must select an appropriate scale.

# Terminology

Note:  This module is a synthesis of concepts learned in all of Grade 9.

## New or Recently Introduced Terms

- **Analytic model** (A model that seeks to explain data based on deeper theoretical ideas.  For example, by using an algebraic equation. This is sometimes referred to as a symbolic model.)
- **Descriptive model** (A model that seeks to describe phenomena or summarize them in a compact form.  For example, by using a graph.)

## Familiar Terms and Symbols[11]

- Function
- Range
- Parent function
- Linear Function
- Quadratic Function
- Exponential Function
- Average Rate of Change
- Cube root function
- Square root function
- End behavior
- Recursive process
- Piecewise Defined Function
- Parameter
- Arithmetic Sequence
- Geometric Sequence
- First Differences
- Second Differences
- Analytical model

# Suggested Tools and Representations

- Scientific calculator
- Graphing calculator
- Geometer's Sketch Pad
- GeoGebra

---

[11] These are terms and symbols students have seen previously.

Module 5:      A Synthesis of Modeling with Equations and Functions
Date:            10/4/13

## Assessment Summary

| Assessment Type | Administered | Format | Standards Addressed |
|---|---|---|---|
| End-of-Module Assessment Task | After Topic B | Constructed response with rubric | N-Q.A.2, N-Q.A.3, A-CED.A.1, A-CED.A.2, F-IF.B.4, F-IF.B.5, F-IF.B.6, F-BF.A.1, F-LE.A.1, F-LE.A.2 |

## Topic A:

# Elements of Modeling

**N-Q.A.2, A-CED.A.2, F-IF.B.4, F-IF.B.5, F-BF.A.1a, F-LE.A.1b, F-LE.A.1c, F-LE.A.2**

| **Focus Standard:** | N-Q.A.2 | Define appropriate quantities for the purpose of descriptive modeling. |
|---|---|---|
| | A-CED.A.2 | Create equations in two or more variables to represent relationships between quantities; graph equations on coordinate axes with labels and scales.★ |
| | F-IF.B.4 | For a function that models a relationship between two quantities, interpret key features of graphs and tables in terms of the quantities, and sketch graphs showing key features given a verbal description of the relationship. *Key features include: intercepts; intervals where the function is increasing, decreasing, positive, or negative; relative maximums and minimums; symmetries; end behavior; and periodicity.*★ |
| | F-IF.B.5 | Relate the domain of a function to its graph and, where applicable, to the quantitative relationship it describes. For example, if the function h(n) gives the number of person-hours it takes to assemble n engines in a factory, then the positive integers would be an appropriate domain for the function.★ |
| | F-BF.A.1a | Write a function that describes a relationship between two quantities.★ |
| | | a. Determine an explicit expression, a recursive process, or steps for calculation from a context. |
| | F-LE.A.1b | Distinguish between situations that can be modeled with linear functions and with exponential functions.★ |
| | F-LE.A.1c | |
| | | b. Recognize situations in which one quantity changes at a constant rate per unit interval relative to another. |
| | | c. Recognize situations in which a quantity grows or decays by a constant percent rate per unit interval relative to another. |
| | F-LE.A.2 | Construct linear and exponential functions, including arithmetic and geometric sequences, given a graph, a description of a relationship, or two input-output pairs (include reading these from a table).★ |

| **Instructional Days:** | 3 |
| --- | --- |
| **Lesson 1:** | Analyzing a Graph |
| **Lesson 2:** | Analyzing a Data Set |
| **Lesson 3:** | Analyzing a Verbal Description |

Topic A deals with some foundational skills in the modeling process. With each lesson, students build a "toolkit" for modeling. They develop fluency in analyzing graphs, data sets, and verbal descriptions of situations for the purpose of modeling; recognizing different function types (e.g., linear, quadratic, exponential, square root, cube root, and absolute value); and identifying the limitations of the model. From each graph, data set, or verbal description, students will recognize the function type and formulate a model, but stop short of solving problems, making predictions, or interpreting key features of functions or solutions. This topic focuses on the skill building required for the lessons in Topic B, where students will take a problem through the complete modeling cycle. This module will deal with both "descriptive models" (such as graphs) and "analytic models" (such as algebraic equations).

In Lesson 1, students recognize the function type represented by a graph. They recognize the key features of linear, quadratic, exponential, cubic, absolute value, piecewise, square root, and cube root functions. These key features include, but are not limited to, the $x$- and $y$-intercepts, vertex, axis of symmetry, and domain and range, as well as domain restrictions dependent on context. They then use the key features and/or data pairs from the graph to create or match to an equation that can be used as another representation of the function; some examples will be in real-world contexts.

Lesson 2 follows the same blueprint. Instead of a graph, students are given a data set presented as a table and asked to identify the function type based on their analysis of the given data. In particular, students look for patterns in the data set at fixed intervals to help them determine the function type, e.g., while linear functions have constant first differences (rate of change), quadratic functions have constant second differences (rate of the rate of change), and exponential functions have a common ratio (constant percent change).

Lesson 3 asks students to make sense of a contextual situation presented as a word problem or as a situation described verbally. They start by making sense of the problem by looking for entry points, analyzing the givens and constraints, and defining the quantities and the relationships described in the context. They recognize specific situations where linear, quadratic, or exponential models are typically used.

# Lesson 1: Analyzing a Graph

## Student Outcomes

- From a graphic representation, students recognize the function type, interpret key features of the graph, and create an equation or table to use as a model of the context for functions addressed in previous modules (i.e., linear, exponential, quadratic, cubic, square root, cube root, absolute value, and other piecewise functions).

## Lesson Notes

This lesson asks students to recognize a function type from a graph, from the function library studied this year (i.e., linear, exponential, quadratic, cubic, square root, cube root, absolute value, and other piecewise functions), and formulate an analytical/symbolic model. For this lesson, students do not go beyond the second step in the modeling cycle, focusing instead on recognition and formulation only. Unlike in previous modules, no curriculum clues are provided (e.g., Lesson or Module title) to guide students toward the type of function represented by the graph. There will be a mix of function types, and students will learn to recognize the clues that are in the graph itself. They will analyze the relationship between the variables and key features of the graph and/or the context to identify the function type. Key features include: the overall shape of the graph (to identify the function type), $x$- and $y$-intercepts (to identify zeros and initial conditions of the function), symmetry, vertices (to identify minimum/maximum values of the function), end behavior, slopes of line segments between two points (to identify average rates of change over intervals), sharp corners or cusps (to identify potential piecewise functions), and gaps or indicated end points (to identify domain and range restrictions).

Throughout this module, teachers should refer to the modeling cycle below (found on page 61 of the CCLS and 72 of the CCSS):

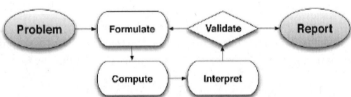

[Note: Writing in a math journal/notebook is suggested for this lesson and all of Module 5. Encourage students to keep and use their journal as a reference throughout the module.]

**Standards for Mathematical Practice:** The opening and discussion for this lesson involve students learning skills important to the modeling cycle. When presented with a problem they will make sense of the given information, analyze the presentation, define the variables involved, look for entry points to a solution, and create an equation to be used as an analytical model.

Classwork

**Opening (8 minutes)**

The opening discussion assumes students have already filled out the Function Summary Chart. Unless you have time to allow for students to work on the chart during class, it would be best to assign the chart as the Problem Set the night before this lesson so that this opening discussion can be a discussion of the students' responses. If time allows, you might use two days for this lesson, with the first day spent discussing the Function Summary Chart, and the second day starting with Example 1.

Have students work independently, but allow them to confer with a partner or small group as they fill in the chart below. Remember that students studied many of these functions earlier in the year and their memories may need to be refreshed. As needed, remind them of the key features that could provide evidence for the function types. Try to keep this exercise to about one minute per graph. You might even set a timer and have students come up with as many features as possible in one minute. Allow them to include the table in their journals/notebooks, as a reference, and to add to it as they work through this lesson and subsequent lessons in this module. The descriptions provided in the third column of the chart are not meant to be exhaustive. Students may have fewer or more observations than the chart provides. Observations may be related to the parent function, but should also take into account the key features of transformations of the parent.*

[*Note: In the table on page 4, and later in this module, the cubic functions we are exploring are basic transformations of the parent function only. We do not yet delve into the study of the general cubic function. The descriptions in the table on page 4 relate to features of basic cubic function and its transformations only, i.e., vertical/horizontal translation AND/OR vertical/horizontal scaling.]

*Scaffolding:*

- Using a visual "journal" of the function families will help struggling students to conceptualize the various functions in their growing library, and to more readily recognize those functions.

- For accelerated students who may need a challenge, ask them to explore cubic functions in factored form and comment on the differences in the key features of those graphs as compared to the basic parent cubic functions. For example, explore the key features of this cubic graph:

$$f(x) = (x - 2)(x + 1)(x - 4)$$

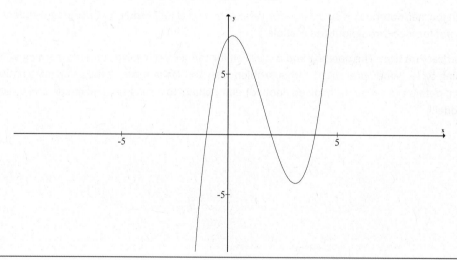

**Opening Exercise**

The graphs below give examples for each parent function we have studied this year. For each graph, identify the function type, and the general form of the parent function's equation; then offer general observations on the key features of the graph that helped you identify the function type. (Function types include: linear, quadratic, exponential, square root, cube root, cubic, absolute value, and other piecewise functions. Key features may include the overall shape of the graph, $x$- and $y$-intercepts, symmetry, a vertex, end behavior, domain and range values/restrictions, and average rates of change over an interval.)

**FUNCTION SUMMARY CHART**

| Graph | Function Type and Parent Function | Function Clues: Key Features, observations |
|---|---|---|
| | *Linear* $f(x) = x$ | *Overall shape is straight line; generally there is one intercept for each axis, except in the case where the slope is 0; in this graph of the parent function, the $x$- and $y$-intercept are the same point, $(0,0)$; the average rate of change is the same for every interval; If a line is horizontal it is still a function (slope is 0), but not if it is vertical; there is no symmetry.* |
| | *Absolute value* $f(x) = |x|$ | *Overall shape is a V; has a vertex – minimum or maximum value depending on the sign of the leading coefficient; the domain is all real numbers, and the range will vary; average rates of change are constant for all intervals with endpoints on the same side of the vertex; either goes up or down to infinity; reflects across a line of symmetry at the vertex; may have one, two, or no $x$-intercepts, and always has one $y$-intercept; this is actually a linear piecewise function.* |
| | *Exponential* $f(x) = a^x$ | *Overall shape is growth or decay function; for the parent shown here (growth), as $x$ increases, $y$ increases more quickly; for decay functions, as $x$ increases, $y$ decreases; domain: $x$ is all real numbers, the range varies but is limited. For this growth parent, $y$ is always greater than 0; for the decay parent, $y$ is always less than 0; for growth/decay functions with a vertical shift, $y$ will be greater than or less than the value of the shift; the parent growth/decay function has no $x$-intercepts (no zeros), but those with a vertical shift will have one $x$- and one $y$-intercept; there is no minimum/maximum value, even though there will be range restrictions for growth, the average rate of change increases as the intervals move to the right; the average rate of change can never be 0; there is no symmetry.* |

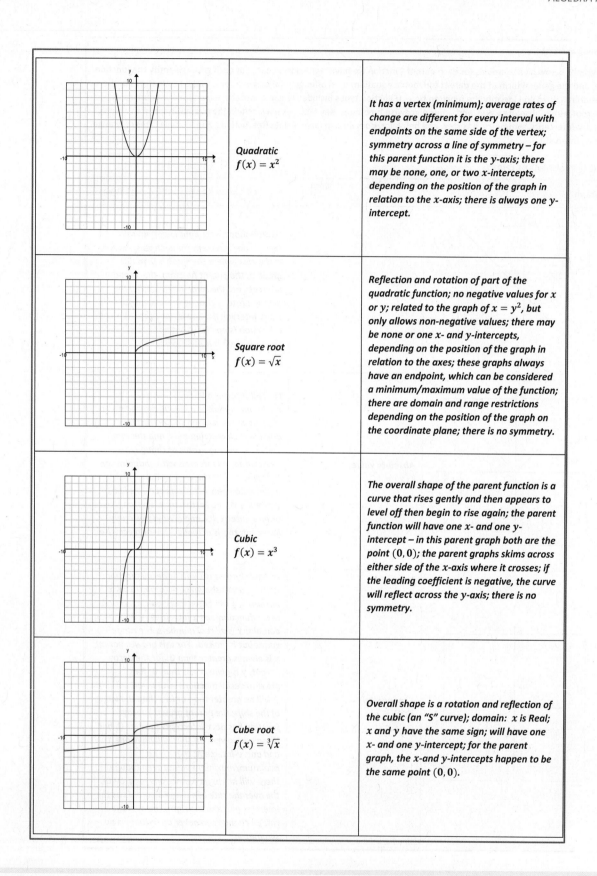

| | Quadratic $f(x) = x^2$ | It has a vertex (minimum); average rates of change are different for every interval with endpoints on the same side of the vertex; symmetry across a line of symmetry – for this parent function it is the y-axis; there may be none, one, or two x-intercepts, depending on the position of the graph in relation to the x-axis; there is always one y-intercept. |
| | Square root $f(x) = \sqrt{x}$ | Reflection and rotation of part of the quadratic function; no negative values for x or y; related to the graph of $x = y^2$, but only allows non-negative values; there may be none or one x- and y-intercepts, depending on the position of the graph in relation to the axes; these graphs always have an endpoint, which can be considered a minimum/maximum value of the function; there are domain and range restrictions depending on the position of the graph on the coordinate plane; there is no symmetry. |
| | Cubic $f(x) = x^3$ | The overall shape of the parent function is a curve that rises gently and then appears to level off then begin to rise again; the parent function will have one x- and one y-intercept – in this parent graph both are the point $(0, 0)$; the parent graphs skims across either side of the x-axis where it crosses; if the leading coefficient is negative, the curve will reflect across the y-axis; there is no symmetry. |
| | Cube root $f(x) = \sqrt[3]{x}$ | Overall shape is a rotation and reflection of the cubic (an "S" curve); domain: x is Real; x and y have the same sign; will have one x- and one y-intercept; for the parent graph, the x-and y-intercepts happen to be the same point $(0, 0)$. |

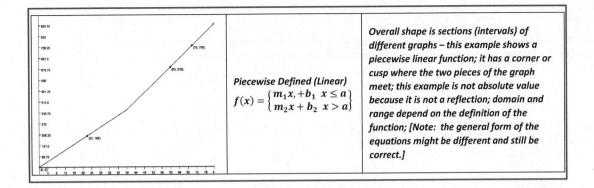

*Piecewise Defined (Linear)*
$$f(x) = \begin{cases} m_1 x, + b_1 & x \le a \\ m_2 x + b_2 & x > a \end{cases}$$

*Overall shape is sections (intervals) of different graphs – this example shows a piecewise linear function; it has a corner or cusp where the two pieces of the graph meet; this example is not absolute value because it is not a reflection; domain and range depend on the definition of the function; [Note: the general form of the equations might be different and still be correct.]*

Hold a short discussion about the charts in the Opening Exercise. Have students refer to their charts to answer the questions below and add to their charts as they gain insights from the discussion. Let them know that this chart will be their reference tool as they work on the lessons in this module. Encourage students to fill it out as completely as possible and to add relevant notes to their math notebooks/journals.

- When presented with a graph, what is the most important key feature that will help you recognize the type of function it represents?
  - *Overall shape is the most readily apparent feature of each function.*
- Which graphs have a minimum/maximum value?
  - *Quadratic, absolute value, square root, and some piecewise functions.*
- Which have domain restrictions? What are those restrictions?
  - *Square root (no negative numbers allowed under the radical), and sometimes piecewise (with defined restrictions in the domains).*
- Which will have restrictions on their range?
  - *Square root, absolute value, exponential, quadratic, and sometimes piecewise.*
- Which have lines of symmetry?
  - *Absolute value, quadratic.*
- Which of the parent functions are transformations of other parent functions?
  - *Cubic and cube root, quadratic and square root.*
- How are you able to recognize the function if the graph is a transformation of the parent function?
  - *The overall shape will be the same, even though sometimes it is shifted (vertically or horizontally), stretched/shrunk, and/or reflected.*

## Example 1 (8 minutes)

Project the graph that follows onto the board or screen. Make sure it is enlarged so that the coordinates are visible. Have students look closely at the piecewise function and talk them through the questions. Leave the graph on the screen while they work on Exercise 1, but discourage them from looking ahead.

Piecewise defined functions have the most variety of all the graphs you have studied this year. Let's look more closely at the piecewise function in your chart in the Opening:

**Example 1**

Eduardo has a summer job that pays him a certain rate for the first 40 hours each week and time-and-a-half for any overtime hours. The graph below shows how much money he earns as a function of the hours he works in one week.

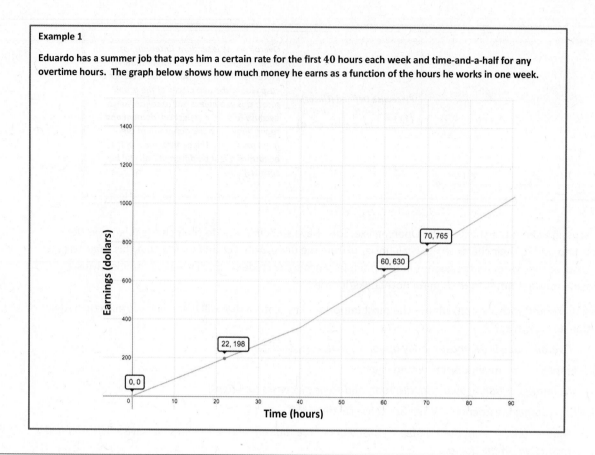

*Scaffolding:*

If students are unable to recognize the correct function for the piecewise graph, write the four functions shown below on the screen or board near the graph and have the students consider each for a few seconds. Then, ask the questions that follow to guide the discussion.

- Which of these general functions below could be used to represent the graph above? How did you choose?

  A: $n(x) = a|x - h| + k$

  B: $v(x) = ax^2 + bx + c$

  C: $g(x) = \begin{cases} m_1 x + b_1, & \text{if } x \le 40 \\ m_2 x + b_2, & \text{if } x > 40 \end{cases}$

  D: $z(x) = mx + b$

  - *C: $g(x)$. The graph is a piecewise function, so the only function that could be correct is a pair of expressions on different intervals of the domain.*

Start by asking students to consider the function equation for this graph and ask them to justify their choice. If students are unable to come up with viable options, you might use this scaffolding suggestion. Otherwise skip to the questions that follow, and use them to guide the discussion. Try to use as little scaffolding as possible in this section so that students have an experience closer to a true modeling situation.

- Right now we are in the *formulate* stage of the modeling cycle. This means we are starting with a *problem,* and selecting a model (symbolic/analytical, tabular, and/or graphic) that can represent the relationship between the variables used in the context. What are the variables in this problem? What are the units?

  - *Time worked (in hours); earnings (in dollars)*

- We have identified the variables. Now let's think about how the problem defines the relationship between the variables.

  - *The number of dollars earned is dependent on the number of hours worked. The relationship is piecewise linear because the average rate of change is constant for each of the intervals (pieces), as depicted in the graph.*

- So what does this graph tell you about Eduardo's pay for his summer job?

  - *He has a constant pay rate up to $40$ hours and then the rate changes to a higher amount. [Students may notice that his pay rate from $0$ to $40$ hours is $9$, and from $40$ hours on is $13.50$.]*

- The graph shows us the relationship. In fact, it is an important part of the *formulating* step because it helps us to better understand the relationship. Why would it be important to find the analytical representation of the function as well?

  - *The equation captures the essence of the relationship succinctly, and allows us to find or estimate values that are not shown on the graph.*

- How did you choose the function type? What were the clues in the graph?

  - *Visually, the graph looks like two straight line segments stitched together. So we can use a linear function to model each straight line segment. The presence of a sharp corner usually indicates a need for a piecewise definition.*

- There are four points given on the graph. Is that enough to determine the function?

  - *In this case, yes. Each linear piece of the function has two points, so we could determine the equation for each.*

- What do you notice about the pieces of the graph?

  - *The second piece is steeper than the first; they meet where $x = 40$; the first goes through the origin; there are two known points for each piece.*

## Exercise 1 (8 minutes)

Have students use the graph in Example 1 to find the function that represents the graph. They should work in pairs or small groups. Circulate throughout the room to make sure all students are able to create a linear equation of each piece.

---

**Exercises**

1.  **Write the function in analytical (symbolic) form for the graph in Example 1.**

    a.  **What is the equation for the first piece of the graph?**

    *The two points we know are $(0, 0)$ and $(22, 198)$. The slope of the line is $9$ (or $9$/hour), and the equation is* $f(x) = 9x.$

---

**b.**  **What is the equation for the second piece of the graph?**

*The second piece has the points* $(60, 630)$ *and* $(70, 765)$*. The slope of the line is* $13.5$ *(or $13.50/hour) and the equation in point-slope form would be either* $y - 630 = 13.5(x - 60)$ *or* $y - 765 = 13.5(x - 70)$*, with both leading to the function,* $f(x) = 13.5x - 180$

**c.**  **What are the domain restrictions for the context?**

*The graph is restricted to one week of work with the first piece starting at* $x = 0$*, and* $x$ *stopping at* $x = 40$*. The second piece applies to* $x$*-values greater than or equal to* $41$*. Since there are* $168$ *hours in one week, the absolute upper limit should be* $168$ *hours. However, no one can work non-stop, so setting* $80$ *hours as an upper limit would be reasonable. Beyond* $168$ *hours, Eduardo would be starting the next week and would start over with $9/hour for the next* $40$ *hours.*

**d.**  **Explain the domain in the context of the problem.**

*The first piece starts at* $x = 0$ *and stops at* $x = 40$*. The second piece starts at* $x \geq 41$*. From* $0$ *to* $40$ *hours the rate is the same: $9/hour. Then, the rate changes to $13.50/hour at* $x \geq 41$*. After* $80$ *hours it is undefined since Eduardo would need to sleep.*

[Note:  Students may notice that the context may not be graphed as precisely as possible, since it is not known for sure whether Eduardo will be paid for partial hours.  However, this would typically be the case.  With the use of a time clock, pay would be to the nearest minute, (i.e., for 30 minutes of work he would get $4.50.)  This could inspire a good discussion about precision in graphing and would show that your students are really thinking mathematically.  You may or may not decide to broach that subject depending on the needs of your students.]


## Exercises 2–6 (10 minutes)

- Graphs are used to represent a function and to model a context.  What would the advantage be to writing an equation to model the situation, too?
    - *With a graph you have to estimate values that are not integers.  Having an equation allows you to evaluate for any domain value and determine the exact value of the function.  Also, with an equation you can more easily extend the function to larger domain and range values – even to those that would be very difficult to capture in a physical graph.  This feature is very useful, for example, in making predictions about the future or extrapolations into the past based on existing graphs of recent data.*

Use the following exercises either as guided or group practice.  For now, we are just building a knowledge base for formulating an equation that matches a graphic model.  Remember that in later lessons we will be applying the functions from a context and taking the problems through the full modeling cycle.  Remind students that using graphs often requires estimation of values, and that using transformations of the parent function can help us create the equation more efficiently.  If needed, offer students some hints and reminders for exponential and absolute value functions. If time is short select, the 2 to 3 graphs below that are likely to prove most challenging for your students (maybe the exponential and cubic or cube root), and assign the rest as part of the Problem Set.

Point out:  Phenomena that occur in real life situations are usually not as tidy as these examples.  We are working on the skills needed to formulate a model and, for the sake of practice, will begin with mathematical functions that are friendly, and not in a context.  Later, we will use more complex and real situations.

For each graph below, use the questions and identified ordered pairs to help you formulate an equation to represent it.

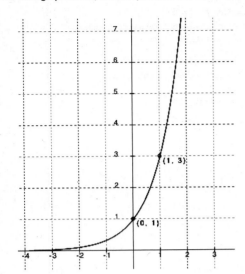

2. **Function type:** Exponential

   **Parent function:** $f(x) = a^x$

   **Transformations:** It appears that the graph could be that of a parent function because it passes through $(0, 1)$, and the $x$-axis is a horizontal asymptote.

   **Equation:** The fact that the graph passes through the point $(0, 1)$, and the $x$-axis is a horizontal asymptote, indicates there is no stretch factor or translation.

   *Finding* a *using* $(1, 3)$:

   $3 = a^1$

   $3 = a$

   *so,* $f(x) = 3^x$

3. **Function type:** *Square root*

   **Parent function:** $f(x) = \sqrt{x}$

   **Transformations:** *Appears to be a stretch*

   **Equation:** $f(x) = a\sqrt{x}$

   *Checking for stretch/shrink factor using* $(4, 4)$:

   $4 = a\sqrt{4}$

   $4 = a(2)$

   $2 = a$

   *Checking* $a = 2$ *with* $(1, 2)$:

   $2 = 2\sqrt{1}$

   $2 = 2$ *Yes!*

   $f(x) = 2\sqrt{x}$

   *[Note: Students may need a hint for this parent function since they have not worked much with square root functions. Also, the stretch factor could be inside or outside the radical. You might ask students who finish early to try it both ways and verify that the results are the same (i.e., use $f(x)) = a\sqrt{x}$ OR $f(x) = \sqrt{bx}$ ).]*

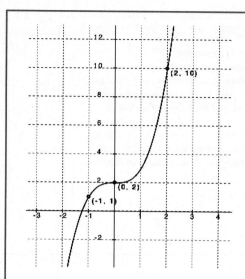

4. **Function type:** *Cubic*
   **Parent function:** $f(x) = x^3$
   **Transformations:** *Appears to be a vertical shift of 2 with no horizontal shift*
   **Equation:** $f(x) = ax^3 + 2$

   *Checking for stretch/shrinking with* $(1, 3)$*:*
   $3 = a(1) + 2$
   $1 = a$ *(no stretches)*

   *Checking with* $(2, 10)$*:*
   $10 = (2)^3 + 2$
   $10 = 8 + 2$
   $10 = 10$ *Yes!*
   $f(x) = x^3 + 2$

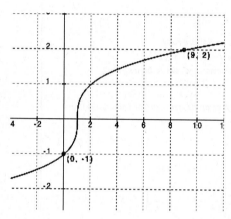

5. **Function type:** *Cube root*
   **Parent function:** $f(x) = \sqrt[3]{x}$
   **Transformations:** *Appears to be a shift to the right of 1*
   **Equation:** $f(x) = \sqrt[3]{x - 1}$

   *Checking for possible stretch/shrinking using* $(9, 2)$*:*
   $2 = \sqrt[3]{9 - 1}$
   $2 = 2$ *Yes!*

   *Now check* $(0, -1)$*:*
   $-1 = \sqrt[3]{0 - 1}$
   $-1 = -1$ *Yes!*
   *So,* $f(x) = \sqrt[3]{x - 1}$ *is the function model.*

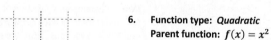

6. **Function type:** *Quadratic*
   **Parent function:** $f(x) = x^2$
   **Transformations:** *Shift up 2 units and to the right 1 unit*
   **Equation:** *Using the vertex form with* $(1, 2)$*:*
   $f(x) = a(x - 1)^2 + 2$

   *Finding the stretch/shrink factor using* $(0, 5)$*:*
   $5 = a(0 - 1)^2 + 2$
   $3 = a(1)$
   $a = 3$

   *Checking with* $(2, 5)$*:*
   $5 = 3(2 - 1)^2 + 2$
   $3 = 3(2 - 1)$
   $3 = 3(1)$ *Yes! There is a stretch factor of 3.*
   $f(x) = 3(x - 1)^2 + 2$

## Closing (3 minutes)

- When given a context is represented graphically, you must first:
  - Identify the variables in the problem (dependent and independent), and
  - Identify the relationship between the variables that are described in the graph/situation.
- To come up with a modeling expression from a graph, you must recognize the type of function the graph represents, observe key features of the graph (including restrictions on the domain), identify the quantities and units involved, and create an equation to analyze the graphed function.
- Identifying a parent function, and thinking of the transformation of the parent function to the graph of the function, can help with creating the analytical representation of the function.

---

**Lesson Summary**

- When given a context represented graphically, you first need to:
  - Identify the variables in the problem (dependent and independent), and
  - Identify the relationship between the variables that are described in the graph/situation.
- To come up with a modeling expression from a graph, you must recognize the type of function the graph represents, observe key features of the graph (including restrictions on the domain), identify the quantities and units involved, and create an equation to analyze the graphed function.
- Identifying a parent function and thinking of the transformation of the parent function to the graph of the function can help with creating the analytical representation of the function.

---

## Exit Ticket (8 minutes)

[Note: Enlarging and displaying the graph for this Exit Ticket problem on the board or screen may be helpful and would be important for student with visual impairments.]

Name _____    Date_____

# Lesson 1:  Analyzing a Graph

Exit Ticket

Read the problem description and answer the questions below.  Use a separate piece of paper if needed.

A library posted a graph in its display case to illustrate the relationship between the fee for any given late day for a borrowed book and the total number of days the book is overdue.  The graph, shown below, includes a few data points for reference.  Rikki has forgotten this policy and wants to know what her fine would be for a given number of late days.

*[Note:  The ordered pairs may be difficult to read.  They are:*  $(1, 0.1)$ $(10, 1)$  *and*  $(11, 1.5)$ $(14, 3)$.*]*

1.   What type of function is this?

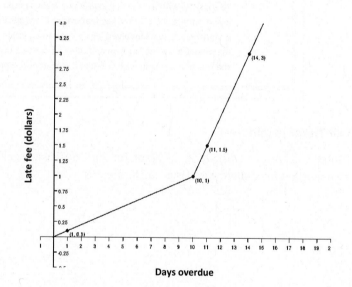

2.   What is the general form of the parent function(s) of this graph?

3.   What equations would you expect to use to model this context?

4.   Describe verbally what this graph is telling you about the library fees.

5.  Compare the advantages and disadvantages of the graph versus the equation as a model for this relationship. What would be the advantage of using a verbal description in this context? How might you use a table of values?

6.  What suggestions would you make to the library for how they could better share this information with their customers? Comment on the accuracy and helpfulness of this graph.

## Exit Ticket Sample Solutions

A library posted a graph in its display case to illustrate the relationship between the fee for any given late day for a borrowed book and the total number of days the book is overdue. The graph is shown below. Rikki has forgotten this policy and wants to know what her fine would be for a given number of late days.

*[Note: The ordered pairs may be difficult to read. They are: $(1, 0.1)$ $(10, 1)$ and $(10, 1)$ $(11, 1.5)$ $(14, 3)$.]*

1. **What type of function is this?**

   *Piecewise linear.*

2. **What is the general form of the parent function(s) of this graph?**

   $$f(x) = \begin{cases} m_1 x, + b_1 & x \le a \\ m_2 x + b_2 & x > a \end{cases}$$

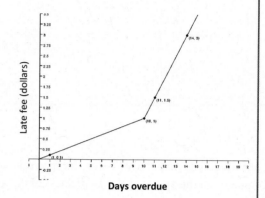

Days overdue

3. **What equations would you expect to use to model this context?**

   $$f(x) = \begin{cases} 0.1x, & if \ x \le 10 \\ 0.5(x - 10) + 1, & if \ x > 10 \end{cases}$$

   *Students may be more informal in their descriptions of the function equation and might choose to make the domain restriction of the second piece inclusive rather than the first piece, since both pieces are joined at the same point. (Remember that only one domain interval can be inclusive at the junction of the pieces.)*

4. **Describe verbally what this graph is telling you about the library fees.**

   *The overdue fee is a flat rate of $\$0.10$ per day for the first 10 days, and then increases to $\$0.50$ per day after 10 days. The fee for each of the first 10 days is $\$0.10$, so the fee for 10 full days is $\$0.10(10) = \$1.00$. Then, the fee for 11 full days of late fees is $\$1.00 + \$0.50 = \$1.50$, etc. (From then on, the fee increases to $\$0.50$ for each additional day.)*

5. **Compare the advantages and disadvantages of the graph versus the equation as a model for this relationship. What is the advantage of using a verbal description in this context? How might you use a table of values?**

   *Graphs are visual and allow us to see the general shape and direction of the function. However, equations allow us to determine more exact values, since graphs only allow for estimates for any non-integer values. The late-fee scenario depends on integer number of days only; other scenarios may involve independent variables of non-integer values (e.g., gallons of gasoline purchased). In this case, a table could be used to show the fee for each day but could also show the accumulated fees for the total number of days. For example, for 15 days the fees would be $\$1.00$ for the first 10 + $\$2.50$ for the next 5, for a total of $\$3.50$.*

6. **What suggestions would you make to the library about how they could better share this information with their customers? Comment on the accuracy and helpfulness of this graph.**

   *Rather than displaying the late fee system in a graph, a table showing the total fine for the number of days late would be clearer. If a graph is preferred, it might be better to use a discrete graph, or even a step graph, since the fees are not figured by the hour or minute but only by the full day. While the given graph shows the rate for each day, most customers would rather know, at a glance, what they owe, in total, for their overdue book.*

## Problem Set Sample Solutions

This problem allows for more practice with writing quadratic equations from a graph. Suggest that students use the vertex form for the equation, as it is the most efficient when the vertex is known. Remind them to always use a second point to find the leading coefficient. (And it is nice to have a third to check their work.)

---

1. During tryouts for the track team, Bob is running 90-foot wind sprints by running from a starting line to the far wall of the gym and back. At time $t = 0$, he is at the starting line and ready to accelerate toward the opposite wall. As $t$ approaches 6 seconds he must slow down, stop for just an instant to touch the wall, turn around, and sprint back to the starting line. His distance, in feet, from the starting line with respect to the number of seconds that has passed for one repetition is modeled by the graph below.

   a. What are the key features of this graph?

   *The graph appears to represent a quadratic function. The maximum point is at $(6, 90)$. The zeros are at $(0, 0)$ and $(12, 0)$.*

   b. What are the units involved?

   *Distance is measured in feet, and time in seconds.*

   c. What is the parent function of this graph?

   *We will attempt to model the graph with a quadratic function. The parent function could be: $f(t) = t^2$.*

   d. Were any transformations made to the parent functions to get this graph?

   *It has a negative leading coefficient and it appears to shift up 90 units, and to the right 6 units.*

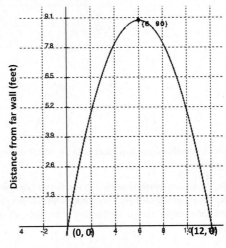

   e. What general analytical representation would you expect to model this context?

   $f(t) = a(t - h)^2 + k$

   f. What do you already know about the parameters of the equation?

   $a < 0, h = 6, k = 90$

   g. Use the ordered pairs you know to replace the parameters in the general form of your equation with constants so that the equation will model this context. Check your answer using the graph.

   *To find $a$, substitute $(0, 0)$ for $(x, y)$ and $(6, 90)$ for $(h, k)$:*

   $$0 = a(0 - 6)^2 + 90$$
   $$-90 = a(36)$$
   $$a = -\frac{90}{36} = -2.5$$
   $$f(t) = -2.5(t - 6)^2 + 90$$

   *Now check it with $(12, 0)$*

   $$0 = -2.5(12 - 6)^2 + 90$$
   $$-90 = -2.5(36)$$
   $$-90 = -90$$

   *Yes!*

---

2.   Spencer and McKenna are on a long-distance bicycle ride.  Spencer leaves one hour before McKenna.  The graph below shows each rider's distance in miles from his or her house as a function of time since McKenna left on her bicycle to catch up with Spencer.  (Note:  Parts (e), (f), and (g) are challenge problems.)

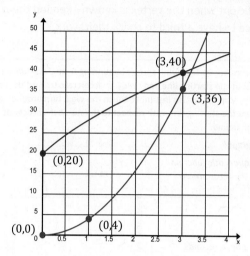

a.   Which function represents Spencer's distance?  Which function represents McKenna's distance?  Explain your reasoning.

*The function that starts at* $(0, 20)$ *represents Spencer's distance since he had a 1-hour head start.  The function that starts at* $(0, 0)$ *represents McKenna's distance since the graph is described as showing distance since she started riding.  That means at the time she started riding* ($t = 0$ *hours), her distance would need to be 0 miles.*

b.   Estimate when McKenna catches up to Spencer.  How far have they traveled at that point in time?

*McKenna will catch up with Spencer after about* $3.25$ *hours.  They will have traveled approximately* $41$ *miles at that point.*

c.   One rider is speeding up as time passes and the other one is slowing down.  Which one is which, and how can you tell from the graphs?

*I know that Spencer is slowing down because his graph is getting less steep as time passes.  I know that McKenna is speeding up because her graph is getting steeper as time passes.*

d.   According to the graphs, what type of function would best model each rider's distance?

*Spencer's graph appears to be modeled by a square root function.  McKenna's graph appears to be quadratic.*

e. Create a function to model each rider's distance as a function of the time since McKenna started riding her bicycle. Use the data points labeled on the graph to create a precise model for each rider's distance.

*If Spencer started 1 hour before McKenna then $(-1, 0)$ would be a point on his graph. Using a square root function in the form $f(x) = k\sqrt{x+1}$ would be appropriate. To find k, substitute $(0, 20)$ into the function.*

$20 = k\sqrt{0+1}$

$20 = k$

*So, $f(x) = 20\sqrt{x+1}$. Check with the other point $(3, 40)$:*

$f(3) = 20\sqrt{3+1}$

$f(3) = 20\sqrt{4} = 40$

*For McKenna, using a quadratic model would mean the vertex must be at $(0, 0)$. A quadratic function in the form $g(x) = kx^2$ would be appropriate. To find k, substitute $(1, 4)$ into the function.*

$4 = k(1)^2$

$4 = k$

*So, $g(x) = 4x^2$. Check with the other point $(3, 36)$: $g(3) = 4(3)^2 = 36$.*

f. What is the meaning of the $x$- and $y$-intercepts of each rider in the context of this problem?

*Spencer's x-intercept $(-1, 0)$ shows that he starts riding one hour before McKenna. McKenna's x-intercept shows that at time 0, her distance from home is 0, which makes sense in this problem. Spencer's y-intercept $(0, 20)$ means that when McKenna starts riding one hour after he begins, he has already traveled 20 miles.*

g. Estimate which rider is traveling faster 30 minutes after McKenna started riding. Show work to support your answer.

*Spencer:*

$\dfrac{f(0.6) - f(0.5)}{0.6 - 0.5} = 8$ *mph.*

*McKenna:*

$\dfrac{g(0.6) - g(0.5)}{0.6 - 0.5} = 4.4$ *mph.*

*Spencer is traveling faster than McKenna 30 minutes after McKenna begins riding because his average rate of change is greater than McKenna's.*

# Lesson 2: Analyzing a Data Set

## Student Outcomes

- Students recognize linear, quadratic, and exponential functions when presented as a data set or sequence, and formulate a model based on the data.

## Lesson Notes

This lesson asks students to use the first steps in the modeling cycle when a mathematical relationship is represented as a table of values. They will look for trends and patterns in the data and formulate a model. First, they will look for common differences between the function values of regular intervals: the first differences for linear, and the second differences for quadratic. For exponential functions, they will look for a common ratio and/or a constant percent change. For this lesson all data will be based on functions' inputs and outputs and the numbers will be "friendly."

Throughout this module refer to the modeling cycle below, (found on page 61 of the CCLS, and page 72 of the CCSS):

**MP.1 & MP.4**

**Standards for Mathematical Practice:** The opening and discussion for this lesson involve students learning to use the first steps in the modeling cycle. When presented with a problem they will make sense of the given information, analyze the presentation, define the variables involved, look for entry points to a solution, and create an equation or graph to model the context. Students represent the data with appropriate symbolic representation and interpret their mathematical results in the context and validate their conclusions.

**MP.8**

**Standards for Mathematical Practice:** All of the examples, exercises and discussion in the lesson require that students search for regularity or trends in tables of values and recognize the correspondence between equations, verbal descriptions and tables.

## Classwork

### Opening (8 minutes)

Display the following three sets of data on the board or screen. Ask students to study each data set and make notes about what they see. Then, have a brainstorming session where students share whatever they observe. Write down all suggestions on the board or screen so that you can come back to them later to see how many were helpful. Use the questions that follow to guide the discussion.

**Opening**

When tables are used to model functions, we typically have just a few sample values of the function, and therefore have to do some detective work to figure out what the function might be. Look at these three tables:

| x | f(x) |
|---|------|
| 0 | 6 |
| 1 | 12 |
| 2 | 18 |
| 3 | 24 |
| 4 | 30 |
| 5 | 36 |

| x | g(x) |
|---|------|
| 0 | 0 |
| 1 | 14 |
| 2 | 24 |
| 3 | 30 |
| 4 | 32 |
| 5 | 30 |

| x | h(x) |
|---|------|
| 0 | 1 |
| 1 | 3 |
| 2 | 9 |
| 3 | 27 |
| 4 | 81 |
| 5 | 243 |

- What do you notice about the three sets of data? Can you identify the type of function they represent? [Students may observe some of the following. It is also possible that they will not notice much of anything or may have ideas that are incorrect. Just let them brainstorm, and then come back to their ideas later to see how many were helpful.] Here are some things they should see:

  - *The orange set is growing much faster than the first two. Many of the function values in the blue and green are the same. It is difficult to know the function by looking at only these numbers for the first two. However, I notice that the function values in the green set were growing steadily, and then decreased at the end. It might help if we had more data points.*

Have students make conjectures about the type of function they believe each data set represents and support their conjecture with evidence, which might include a graph.

Now show a data plot for each:

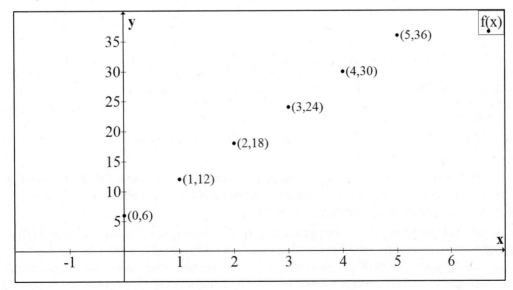

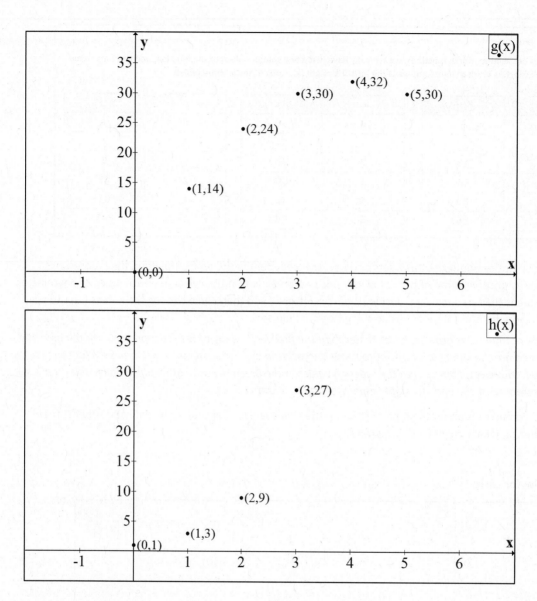

- Now can you see the trends more clearly?

  - *Yes, it is obvious that the first is linear. It is clearer that the second is quadratic. And the third looks to be exponential.*

- We learned to determine the type of function by looking at the shapes of graphs. Can we also determine the type of function by just using its table of values? Analyze each table and find any special patterns that may help determine the type of function it represents.

  - *The table of values for linear function has a constant first difference of 6, indicating the graph will have a slope of 6. The quadratic function does not have a constant difference like a linear function. However, the difference of differences (second difference) is constant. The exponential function does not have constant first or second differences. However, the y-value is multiplied by constant value of 3. It should be noted that the x-values are all increasing by one. Not all data are presented where the x-values are increasing by a constant value, so it is necessary to interpolate values to produce equal-sized intervals.*

## Discussion (10 minutes)

Have students take notes in their math journals/notebooks about the discoveries made in the discussion below. With each guiding question, allow enough time for students to make a journal entry. Encourage them to keep their notes organized, because they may be of later use as a reference tool.

- **How can we identify a linear function from its data?**
  - *First, make sure the $x$-values have a constant difference. Then, check to see if the first differences (changes) between successive $y$-values are constant (i.e., the successive $y$-values are found by adding a constant value).*

- **How can we identify a quadratic function from its data?**
  - *First, make sure the $x$-values have a constant difference. Then, if the first differences are not constant, look to see if the second differences are (i.e., the changes in the changes are constant or the differences between the first differences are constant, and not zero).*

- **How can we identify an exponential function from its data?**
  - *First, make sure the $x$-values have a constant difference. Then, look to see if there is a constant ratio between successive $y$-values (i.e., that the $y$-values are found by multiplying by a constant).*

- **How can we identify an absolute value function from a data set?**
  - *We would notice first that the same phenomenon that happens with a quadratic – the values go up and then down, or vice-versa, if the vertex is included in, or straddled by, the data set. However, when we check for constant first differences, we find them to be constant. That tells us that the pieces of the graph on each side of the minimum/maximum point are parts of lines, and that the data set can be modeled by an absolute value.*

- **How about square root and cube root? How might we recognize them from a set of data?**
  - *For square root, we check to see if squaring the $y$-value results in the corresponding $x$-value. For cube root parent functions, we see if cubing the $y$-value results in the corresponding $x$-value. If the graphs have been transformed, then squaring or cubing the output will not directly yield the input value. One needs to take care of the transformation to identify whether it is a square root or cube root function.*

Make sure students have time to make entries in their math journals before continuing with the following example.

*Scaffolding:*

- Having students keep a math journal/notebook helps to solidify their procedural knowledge-base, and provides more opportunities to deepen their conceptual understanding. Allowing students to use their notebooks as a reference encourages them to be thorough in their note-taking, and improves their attention to and involvement in discussions.

- Occasionally ask a couple of students to share what they have written in their notebooks to give others ideas on how to take good notes.

## Example 1 (8 minutes)

Have the students read the prompt and analyze the data sets for this problem, then have them work with a partner or small group to answer the questions that follow.

**Example 1**

Noam and Athena had an argument about whether it would take longer to get from NYC to Boston and back by car, or by train. To settle their differences, they made separate, non-stop round trips from NYC to Boston. On the trip, at the end of each hour, both recorded the number of miles they had traveled from their starting points in NYC. The tables below show their travel times, in hours, and the distances from their starting points, in miles. The first table shows Noam's travel time/distance from the starting point, and the second represents Athena's. Use *both* data sets to justify your answers to the questions below.

| Time in Hours | Noam's Distance in miles |
|:---:|:---:|
| 0 | 0 |
| 1 | 55 |
| 2 | 110 |
| 3 | 165 |
| 4 | 220 |
| 5 | 165 |
| 6 | 110 |
| 7 | 55 |
| 8 | 0 |

| Time in Hours | Athena's Distance in miles |
|:---:|:---:|
| 0 | 0 |
| 1 | 81 |
| 2 | 144 |
| 3 | 189 |
| 4 | 216 |
| 5 | 225 |
| 6 | 216 |
| 7 | 189 |
| 8 | 144 |
| 9 | 81 |
| 10 | 0 |

*Scaffolding:*

You might want to demonstrate the repeated calculations for the first table (MP.8):

$$0(55) = 0$$
$$1(55) = 55$$
$$2(55) = 110$$

a.  Who do you think is driving, and who is riding the train? Explain your answer in the context of the problem.

*[This is an open-ended question with no right or wrong answer. Check for mathematically sound reasoning based on the data.]*

*Sample Response: It appears that Athena is riding the train since she was able to go 81 miles in the first hour, and Noam was able to go only 55, which is a typical highway speed. Also, Athena made the round trip in 10 hours, while Noam made it in 8, so it looks like the train may have had to stop at stations when it was near Boston, slowing its progress considerably during the 2 hours on either side of Boston.*

b.  According to the data, how far apart are Boston and New York City? Explain mathematically.

*[This is an open-ended question with no right or wrong answer. Check for mathematically sound reasoning based on the data.]*

*Sample Response: Based on the symmetry of the values in the table, Noam's maximum distance was 220 miles (at 4 hours). Using the same symmetry, Athena's maximum value was 225. They may have started or ended at different places, but it is more likely that the route for the train was slightly different than that of the car.*

c. How long did it take each of them to make the round trip?

*Let's call Noam's distance $N(t)$ and Athena's $A(t)$. Noam was traveling for 8 hours, and Athena for 10 hours. The zeros for $N(t)$ are $(0,0)$ and $(8,0)$ and for $A(t)$ are $(0,0)$ and $(10,0)$. It took Noam 8 hours; it took Athena 10 hours.*

d. According to their collected data, which method of travel was faster?

*In this case, the car was faster by 2 hours, overall. However, the speed of the train was faster for the first and the last hour, then slowed.*

e. What was the average rate of change for Athena for the interval from 3 to 4 hours? How might you explain that in the context of the problem?

*She only traveled 27 miles per hour, $\dfrac{216-189}{4-3}$. Since she was likely on the train, there may have been stops during that time period.*

f. Noam believes a quadratic function can be used as a model for both data sets. Do you agree? Use and describe the key features of the functions represented by the data sets to support your answer.

*The two data sets have several things in common. Both are symmetric, both have a vertex, and both have $(0,0)$ as one of the x-intercepts and the y-intercept. The other x-intercept is $(8,0)$ for Noam and $(10,0)$ for Athena. However Noam's data set has a positive constant difference of $+55$ on one side of the vertex, which then changes to $-55$ on the other side. Noam's data set can be best modeled by an absolute value or other piecewise function. Athena's data does not have a constant first difference so is not linear. When we check the second differences we find it to be constant $(18)$. Therefore, Athena's trip can be modeled with a quadratic function.*

> *Scaffolding:*
>
> As an extension for this task you might ask students to create the function equation for each of the data sets.
>
> *Solutions:*
> $N(t) = -55\,|x - 4| + 220$
> OR
> $N(t) = \begin{cases} 55t, & 0 \le t \le 4 \\ -55t + 440, & 4 < t \le 8 \end{cases}$
>
> $A(t) = -9(x-5)^2 + 225$

## Exercises 1–2 (15 minutes)

**Exercises**

1. Explain why each function can or cannot be used to model the given data set:

   a. $f(x) = 3x + 5$

   *This function cannot be used to model the data set. The y-intercept is five, but the first difference is not constant, and the data set is not a linear function.*

   b. $f(x) = -(x - 2)^2 + 9$

   *This function can be used to model the data set. The second difference has a constant value of $-2$; therefore, it is a quadratic function. The vertex is $(2, 9)$ and it is a maximum, since the leading coefficient is negative.*

   | $x$ | $f(x)$ |
   |-----|--------|
   | 0   | 5      |
   | 1   | 8      |
   | 2   | 9      |
   | 3   | 8      |
   | 4   | 5      |
   | 5   | 0      |
   | 6   | $-7$   |

   c. $f(x) = -x^2 + 4x - 5$

   *This function cannot be used to model the data set. The y-intercept for this equation is $-5$ instead of 5.*

**d.** $f(x) = 3^x + 4$

*This function cannot be use used to model the data set. The y-intercept is five, but $f(x)$ values are not being multiplied by a constant value. It is not an exponential function.*

**e.** $f(x) = (x + 2)^2 - 9$

*This function cannot be used to model the data set. The vertex is $(2, 9)$ however it is a minimum in this function.*

**f.** $f(x) = -(x + 1)(x - 5)$

*This function can be used to model the data set. One of the x-intercepts is $x = 5$, and the second x-intercept is $x = -1$ by following the pattern of the data. The function equation indicates x-intercepts of $-1$ and $5$, where the vertex is a maximum value of the function.*

2. Match each table below to the function and the context, and explain how you made your decision.

**A**

| $x$ | $y$ |
|-----|-----|
| 1 | 9 |
| 2 | 18 |
| 3 | 27 |
| 4 | 18 |
| 5 | 9 |

**B**

| $x$ | $y$ |
|-----|-----|
| 1 | 12 |
| 2 | 24 |
| 3 | 36 |
| 4 | 48 |
| 5 | 60 |

**C**

| $x$ | $y$ |
|-----|-----|
| 0 | 160 |
| 1 | 174 |
| 2 | 156 |
| 3 | 106 |
| 4 | 24 |

**D**

| $x$ | $y$ |
|-----|-----|
| 1 | 2 |
| 2 | 4 |
| 3 | 8 |
| 4 | 16 |
| 5 | 32 |

**E**

| $x$ | $y$ |
|-----|-----|
| 2 | 8 |
| 3 | 9 |
| 4 | 8 |
| 5 | 5 |
| 6 | 0 |

Equation *h*
Context **5**

Equation *f*
Context **4**

Equation *q*
Context **2**

Equation *p*
Context **1**

Equation *g*
Context **3**

**Equations:**

$$f(x) = 12x$$

$$h(x) = -9|x - 3| + 27$$

$$g(x) = -(x)(x - 6)$$

$$p(x) = 2^x$$

$$q(x) = -16x^2 + 30x + 160$$

**Contexts:**

1. The population of bacteria doubled every month and the total population vs. time was recorded.

2. A ball was launched upward from the top of a building and the vertical distance of the ball from the ground vs. time was recorded.

3. The height of a certain animal's vertical leap was recorded at regular time intervals of one second; the animal returned to ground level after six seconds.

4. Melvin saves the same amount of money every month. The total amount saved after each month was recorded.

5. Chris ran at a constant rate on a straight-line path, and then returned at the same rate. His distance from his starting point was recorded at regular time intervals.

## Closing (3 minutes)

- How do we determine the type of function from a given set of data?
  - If the first difference is constant, then the data set could be modeled by a linear function.
  - If the second difference is constant, then the data set could be modeled by a quadratic function.
  - If each $y$-value is the previous $y$-value multiplied by a constant (and the $x$-values increase by a constant increment), then the data set could be modeled by an exponential function.

---

**Lesson Summary**

The following methods can be used to determine the appropriate model for a given data set as linear, quadratic or exponential function:

- If the first difference is constant, then the data set could be modeled by a linear function.
- If the second difference is constant, then the data set could be modeled by a quadratic function.
- If the subsequent $y$-values are multiplied by a constant, then the data set could be modeled by an exponential function.

---

## Exit Ticket (6 minutes)

Name _____     Date_____

# Lesson 2: Analyzing a Data Set

Exit Ticket

Analyze these data sets, recognizing the unique pattern and key feature(s) for each relationship. Then use your findings to fill in the missing data, match to the correct function from the list on the right, and describe the key feature(s) that helped you choose the function.

**Table A**

| x | y |
|---|---|
| 0 | 6 |
| 1 | 10 |
| 2 | 14 |
| 3 | ◯ |
| 4 | 22 |
| 5 | ◯ |

**Table B**

| x | y |
|---|---|
| 0 | 6 |
| 1 | 15 |
| 2 | 18 |
| 3 | 15 |
| 4 | ◯ |
| 5 | ◯ |

**Table C**

| x | y |
|---|---|
| −1 | $\frac{1}{6}$ |
| 0 | 1 |
| 1 | ◯ |
| 2 | 36 |
| 3 | ◯ |
| 4 | 1296 |

**Table D**

| x | y |
|---|---|
| −1 | ◯ |
| 0 | 6 |
| 1 | 8 |
| 2 | 6 |
| 3 | 0 |
| 4 | ◯ |
| 5 | −24 |

*Equations:*

$$f(x) = 6^x$$

$$h(x) = -3(x-2)^2 + 18$$

$$g(x) = -2(x+1)(x-3)$$

$$r(x) = 4x + 6$$

Table A: _____ Key Feature(s): _____

Table B: _____ Key Feature(s): _____

Table C: _____ Key Feature(s): _____

Table D: _____ Key Feature(s): _____

## Exit Ticket Sample Solutions

Analyze these data sets, recognizing the unique pattern and key feature(s) for each relationship. Then use your findings to fill in the missing data, match to the correct function from the list on the right, and describe the key feature(s) that helped you choose the function.

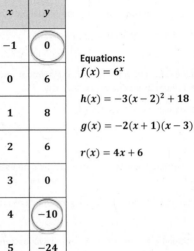

**Table A**

| $x$ | $y$ |
|-----|-----|
| 0 | 6 |
| 1 | 10 |
| 2 | 14 |
| 3 | (18) |
| 4 | 22 |
| 5 | (26) |

**Table B**

| $x$ | $y$ |
|-----|-----|
| 0 | 6 |
| 1 | 15 |
| 2 | 18 |
| 3 | 15 |
| 4 | (6) |
| 5 | (−9) |

**Table C**

| $x$ | $y$ |
|-----|-----|
| −1 | 1/6 |
| 0 | 1 |
| 1 | (6) |
| 2 | 36 |
| 3 | (216) |
| 4 | 1296 |

**Table D**

| $x$ | $y$ |
|-----|-----|
| −1 | (0) |
| 0 | 6 |
| 1 | 8 |
| 2 | 6 |
| 3 | 0 |
| 4 | (−10) |
| 5 | −24 |

**Equations:**

$$f(x) = 6^x$$

$$h(x) = -3(x - 2)^2 + 18$$

$$g(x) = -2(x + 1)(x - 3)$$

$$r(x) = 4x + 6$$

Table A: _____ $r(x)$ _____ Key Feature(s): *Constant slope (first difference) is 4*

Table B: _____ $h(x)$ _____ Key Feature(s): *$(2, 18)$ is the maximum point; Second differences are $-6$*

Table C: _____ $f(x)$ _____ Key Feature(s): *Exponential growth; Common ratio is 6*

Table D: _____ $g(x)$ _____ Key Feature(s): *Includes the x-intercept $(3, 0)$; Second differences are $-4$*

## Problem Set Sample Solutions

**1.**

a. Determine the function type that could be used to model the data set at the right and explain why.

*Quadratic – the second difference is 4.*

b. Complete the data set using the special pattern of the function you described above.

*[See the completed table for answers.]*

c. If it exists, find the minimum or maximum value for the function model. If there is no minimum or maximum, explain why.

*Minimum value occurs at $(4, -8)$.*

| x | y |
|---|---|
| 0 | 24 |
| 1 | 10 |
| 2 | 0 |
| 3 | −6 |
| 4 | −8 |
| 5 | −6 |
| 6 | 0 |

**2.**

a. Determine the function type that could be used to model the data set and explain why.

*Exponential – y-value is being multiplied by constant value 4.*

b. Complete the data set using the special pattern of the function you described above.

*[See responses in the completed table.]*

c. If it exists, find the minimum or maximum value for the function model. If there is no minimum/maximum, explain why.

*Since this is an exponential function, the y-values will increase as x-values increase and there will be no maximum value. As x gets smaller and smaller (i.e., moves further to the left on the number line) the y-values approach 0 but will never reach 0, and never become negative. Therefore, there is no minimum value of this function.*

| x | y |
|---|---|
| −1 | 1/4 |
| 0 | 1 |
| 1 | 4 |
| 2 | 16 |
| 3 | 64 |
| 4 | 256 |
| 5 | 1024 |

**3.**

a. Determine the function type that could be used to model the data set and explain why.

*Linear – the first difference is 6.*

b. Complete the data set using the special pattern of the function you described above.

*[See responses in the completed table.]*

c. If it exists, find the minimal or maximum value for the function model. If there is no minimum/maximum, explain why.

*There is no minimum or maximum value for a linear function (except for a horizontal line). For this function the y-value decreases as the x-value decreases, and the y-value increases as the x-value increases.*

| x | y |
|---|---|
| −1 | 6 |
| 0 | 12 |
| 1 | 18 |
| 2 | 24 |
| 3 | 30 |
| 4 | 36 |
| 5 | 42 |

4. Circle all the function types that could possibly be used to model a context if the given statement applies.

a. When $x$-values are at regular intervals the first difference of $y$-values is not constant.

Linear Function    (Quadratic Function)    (Exponential Function)    (Absolute Value Function)

b. The second difference of data values is not constant.

Linear Function    Quadratic Function    (Exponential Function)    (Absolute Value Function)

c. When $x$-values are at regular intervals, the quotient of any two consecutive $y$-values is a constant that is not equal to $0$ or $1$.

Linear Function    Quadratic Function    (Exponential Function)    Absolute Value Function

d. There maybe two different $x$-values for $y = 0$.

Linear Function    (Quadratic Function)    Exponential Function    (Absolute Value Function)

# Lesson 3: Analyzing a Verbal Description

## Student Outcomes

- Students make sense of a contextual situation that can be modeled with linear, quadratic, and exponential functions when presented as a word problem. They analyze a verbal description and create a model using equations, graphs, or tables.

## Lesson Notes

This lesson asks students to recognize a function type from a verbal description of a context, using linear, quadratic, and exponential functions and linear inequalities. They formulate a model that can be used to analyze the function in its context. For this lesson, they will not go beyond the second step in the modeling cycle but will focus on recognition and formulation only. Unlike in previous modules, no curriculum clues will be provided (e.g., Lesson or Module title) to guide students toward the type of function represented by the situation. There will be a mix of function types and students will learn to recognize the clues that are in the description itself. They will analyze the relationship between the variables and/or the contextual situation to identify the function type.

Throughout this module refer to the modeling cycle below (found on page 61 of the CCLS, and page 72 of the CCSS):

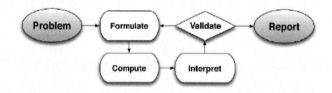

 **Standards for Mathematical Practice:** Throughout this lesson students use the first steps in the modeling cycle. When presented with a problem they will make sense of the given information, define the variables involved, look for entry points to a solution, and create an equation to be used as a model for the context.

**MP.1 & MP.4**

## Classwork

### Opening (15 minutes)

There are a number of everyday problems that we will use for mathematical modeling. It may be helpful to review them quickly before beginning this lesson. Present these on the board or screen and invite students to take notes in their math journals/notebooks. [Note: This Opening is meant to offer suggestions for deciphering descriptions of contextual situations and is not intended to be comprehensive or a list of keywords. Students should use this information to find an entry point to solving a problem, and should not be encouraged to do "keyword reading" of modeling problems.]

> **Scaffolding:**
>
> You might decide to skip this Opening if your students do not need this review.

Rate problems – Linear

Rate problems relate two quantities, usually in different units. Rate problems commonly use some measure of distance and time such as feet per second. These are called *uniform rate* word problems. Rate problems might also use quantities that are not related to distance or time (e.g., pills per bottle, dollars per pound). Rate problems may also relate the number of people to a space (e.g., students per class), the number of objects to a space (e.g., corn stalks per row, or rows of corn per field), dollars per mile (e.g., taxi fare), or dollars per person. The possibilities are limitless, and remember that sometimes the uniform rate problem will include a flat fee plus a rate per unit, making the linear model a bit more interesting.

- The familiar formula, (Rate)(Time) = Distance, can be adjusted to accommodate any (or all) of the uniform rate problem situations mentioned above. These use the equation of the form $f(x) = mx$ (or $d = rt$, etc.).

- Sometimes the rate will be combined with a constant part (e.g., flat fee). For example, a taxi service charges $4 plus $2.50 per mile (times the mileage). These equations will use the form $f(x) = mx + b$.

- These problems might include inequalities, with a maximum or minimum amount possible set by real-life conditions. For example, in a rate problem there may be a minimum number of corn stalks needed in a stalks-per-row problem, or a maximum number of classrooms in a students-per-classroom problem.

- Note: Be careful not to confuse a simple rate problem with one that involves the motion of a free falling object.

Objects in Motion and Area – Quadratic

Motion problems are related to free falling objects[1] or projectiles under the influence of gravity. The functions used to model these functions will always be quadratic and relate the distance from the initial position (i.e., the height from which the object was dropped or projected into the air), measured in either feet or meters, to the time that has passed (i.e., the number of seconds since the object was projected into the air).

In area problems with dimensions that are variable and linear, expressions representing areas will be quadratic.

- When distances are measured in feet, we use: $h(t) = -16t^2 + v_0 t + h_0$, where $h$= height of the object in feet, $t$= time in seconds, $v_0$= initial velocity, and $h_0$= initial position (starting height).

- When distances are measured in meters, we use: $h(t) = -4.9t^2 + v_0 t + h_0$, with all the same variables as above.

- When linear measurements have first degree variables and are used to find area, the result will likely be a quadratic model.

- For rectangular area, $A = (l)(w)$; for triangles, $A = \frac{1}{2}(b)(h)$; for trapezoids, $A = \frac{1}{2}(b_1 + b_2)(h)$. All of these, and many others, can lead to a quadratic function that models the area of the 2-dimensional figure.

Growth problems – Exponential

Exponential problems could involve growth or decay of money (e.g., interest earned or paid), percent growth or decay (e.g., inflation or depreciation), radioactive material (e.g., half-life problems), population (e.g., bacteria, humans, or rabbits), etc.

---

[1] Free falling objects: Objects that are projected, launched, thrown, or dropped, without the aid of a motor (or other device) that provides additional force beyond the initial projection of the object. The object might be shot from a cannon or dropped from a cliff, but will have no rotors, motor, wing, or other device to keep it aloft or defy gravity.

- The general form for any problem related to exponential growth is $f(x) = ab^x$, where $a$ and $b$ are constant values. You can use this form for just about every exponential growth problem, but there are some special cases for which we have special forms of this same function (see the following).
  [Note: Except in problems of compounded interest, encourage students to use the general exponential form for most problems related to growth, as it is usually the most efficient.]

- Depending on how the interest is compounded, we would use different forms of the growth function. Until you get a little further in your math studies, we will use the annual compound interest formula:
  $P(t) = P_0 \left(1 + \frac{r}{n}\right)^{nt}$, where $P$ represents the current or future value of the money, $P_0$ is the principal amount (the initial investment), $r$ is the annual interest rate, $n$ represents the number of times per year the interest is compounded, and $t$ is the number of years the interest is earned or paid.

- Population growth is generally modeled with the general exponential function form. Sometimes it is helpful to know a few commonly used variables : $P(n) = P_0(1 + r)^n$, where $P$ represents the future population, $P_0$ = initial population, $r$ = growth rate, and $n$ is the number of time periods of growth.

- Sometimes in growth problems you need to determine a percentage rate of growth over an interval of time yourself. If that happens, use this strategy: Find the total growth for the interval, $(P - P_0)$ and divide by $P_0$ (the starting population/value), this gives you a ratio representing the new growth to the new population/value. This result will be in decimal form and can be used that way, or changed to a percentage. So, to recap: a percentage rate of growth for an interval can be determined by the expression, $\frac{100(P - P_0)}{P_0}$.

- Point out (or ask): Do you see that all these exponential formulas are really different forms of the general exponential equation in the first bullet? $f(x) = ab^x$? To highlight MP.7, ask students to identify and interpret $a$ and $b$ in the various examples above."

Have students follow the three examples below with a partner or small groups. Give them about 2 minutes to work on the function, and then pause to have the group discuss the suggested questions together. Try to keep this to about 5 minutes per example.

## Example 1 (5 minutes)

Have students read the problem, then use the questions that follow to guide a discussion. Offering a variety of tools for students to use while engaging with these examples will promote MP.5 and also allow multiple entry points for model development. Consider offering access to a graphing calculator, or graphing computer software, graph paper, and a spreadsheet program.

*Scaffolding:*

- Have struggling students keep notes in their math journals/notebooks where all contextual scenarios (and the corresponding functions used) are recorded as the class works through the examples.

- Having this notebook readily available will benefit all students.

> **Example 1**
>
> Gregory plans to purchase a video game player. He has $500 in his savings account, and plans to save $20 per week from his allowance until he has enough money to buy the player. He needs to figure out how long it will take. What type of function should he use to model this problem?

- Gregory decides that the exponential function can best represent the situation. Do you agree or disagree? Why? Support your answer mathematically.

  - *I disagree, because Gregory's money increases at a constant rate of $20 a week with a starting balance of $500. The graph of the amount of money that Gregory saves over a period of time will be a linear model.*

- What are the variables and quantities of this problem?

  - *The rate is $20 per week, w is the number of weeks), and the initial value is $500.*

- What function represents the amount of Gregory's money over a period of time (in weeks)?

  - *The model is $f(w) = 20w + 500$. If the function is graphed, the slope of the line will be 20 to reflect the constant rate of $20/week and the y-intercept will be 500, the initial amount.*

## Example 2 (5 minutes)

---

**Example 2**

One of the highlights in a car show event is a car driving up a ramp and 'flying' over approximately five cars placed end-to-end. The ramp is 8 feet at its highest point, and there is an upward speed of 88 feet per second before it leaves the top of the ramp.

---

- What type of function can best model the height, $h$, in feet, the car travelled in $t$ seconds after leaving the end of the ramp? What were your clues? Justify your answer mathematically.

  - *Quadratic Function, this is an object in motion problem. The car would leave the ramp in an upward and forward motion and then, after travelling higher for a short time, would begin the fall due to the force of gravity.*

- What form would the equation take?

  - *Since the distance is measured in feet and the time in seconds, we would use: $h(t) = -16t^2 + v_0t + h_0$, and the equation would be: $h(t) = -16t^2 + 88t + 8$*

## Example 3 (5 minutes)

---

**Example 3**

Margie got $1000 from her grandmother to start her college fund. She is opening a new savings account and finds out that her bank offers a 2% annual interest rate, compounded monthly.

---

- What type of function would best represent the amount of money in the bank compounded monthly at the rate of 2% per annum? Justify your answer mathematically.

  - *Exponential Function. The amount of deposited money grows over time at a constant rate, and the pattern can be best described by an exponential function, $f(x) = ab^x$, where a represents the initial investment, and b is the expression $\left(1 + \frac{r}{n}\right)$ as defined in the compounded interest formula:*
  
  $$P(t) = P_0\left(1 + \frac{r}{n}\right)^{nt}.$$

- What function represents the amount of money deposited in the bank compounded monthly at the rate of 2%, if the initial amount of deposit was $1000?

  □  $A(n) = 1000 \left(1 + \frac{0.02}{12}\right)^{12n}$

- [Note: We do not know how long Margie plans to leave the money in her account, so we don't know what the value of $n$ is yet.]

Remind students that percentages, in most cases, must be changed to decimals when used in exponential expressions.

### Exercises 1–4 (12 minutes)

Have students work with a partner or small group to determine the function model for the situation described. Circulate around the room to make sure students understand the exercise. If time is short, some of these might be used for additional Problem Set questions.

---

**Exercises**

1. City workers recorded the number of squirrels in a park over a period of time. At the first count, there were 15 pairs of male and female squirrels (30 squirrels total). After 6 months, the scientists recorded a total of 60 squirrels, and after a year, there were 120.

   a. What type of function can best model the population of squirrels recorded over a period of time, assuming the same growth rate and that no squirrel dies?

   *Exponential Function.*

   b. Write a function that represents the population of squirrels recorded over $x$ number of years. Explain how you determined your function.

   *Students may use the general exponential function $f(x) = ab^x$, by figuring out that this is a doubling exponential problem (in this case, the number of squirrels doubles every 6 months). So, the function would be $f(x) = 30(2)^{2x}$, since the squirrel population would double twice each year.*

2. A rectangular photograph measuring 8 inches by 10 inches is surrounded by a frame with a uniform width, $x$.

   a. What type of function can best represent the area of the picture and the frame in terms of $x$ (the unknown frame's width)? Explain mathematically how you know.

   *Quadratic, this is an area problem where the product of two linear measurements will result in a quadratic.*

   b. Write an equation in standard form representing the area of the picture and the frame. Explain how you arrive at your equation.

   *The dimensions of the picture are 8 inches by 10 inches. Taking into consideration the width of the frame, we have to add $x$ to both width and the length of the picture. Doing so results in: $(8 + 2x)$ and $(10 + 2x)$. So, the area of the picture and the frame is: $A(x) = (8 + 2x)(10 + 2x)$, or $A(x) = 4x^2 + 36x + 80$.*

3. A ball is tossed up in the air at an initial rate of 50 feet per second from 5 feet off the ground.

   a. What type of function models the height ($h$, in feet) of the ball after $t$ seconds?

   *Quadratic Function.*

---

Lesson 3: Analyzing a Verbal Description
Date: 10/4/13

b.  Explain what is happening to the height of the ball as it travels over a period of time (in $t$ seconds)?

*The initial height of the ball is 5 ft., and it travels upward with an initial velocity of 50 ft./sec. As time increases, the ball continues to travel upward, with the force of gravity slowing it down, until it reaches the maximum height and falls back to the ground.*

c.  What function models the height, $h$ (in feet), of the ball over a period of time (in $t$ seconds)?

$h(x) = -16t^2 + 50t + 5$

4.  A population of insects is known to triple in size every month. At the beginning of a scientific research project, there were 200 insects.

a.  What type of function models the population of the insects after $t$ years?

*Exponential.*

b.  Write a function that models the population growth of the insects after $t$ years?

*Using the general exponential for tripling a population ($b = 3$), we have the initial population of 200 and $12t$ is the number of growth cycles per year. The function would be $f(t) = 200(3)^{12t}$.*

$P = P_0(1 + r)^{nt}$

$P(x) = 200(1 + 2)^{12t}$, *where r= growth rate at 200% and $n = 12$.*

*So, $P(x) = 200(3)^{12t}$*

## Closing (1 minute)

- How would you know which function to use to model a word problem?

  □ *If the word problem talks about repeatedly adding or subtracting a constant value, then it is linear. If the problem involves motion of objects subject to non-zero, constant acceleration (e.g., gravity) over time or represents an area, then it is quadratic. If the problem is about conventional population growth or compounded interest with a constant growth rate, it is exponential.*

---

**Lesson Summary**

The following methods can be used to recognize a function type from a word problem:

1.  If a problem requires repeated adding or subtracting a constant value, then it is represented by a linear function.
2.  If a problem involves free-falling motion of object or an area, then it is represented by a quadratic function.
3.  If a problem is about population growth or compound interest, then it is represented by an exponential function.

---

## Exit Ticket (2 minutes)

| Lesson 3: | Analyzing a Verbal Description |
|---|---|
| Date: | 10/4/13 |

45

Name _____     Date_____

# Lesson 3:  Analyzing a Verbal Description

Exit Ticket

Create a model to compare these two texting plans:

i.   Plan A costs $15 a month, including 200 free texts.  After 200, they cost $0.15 each.

ii.  Plan B costs $20 a month, including 250 free texts.  After 250, they cost $0.10 each.

## Exit Ticket Sample Solutions

Create a model to compare these two texting plans:

 i.  Plan A costs $15 a month, including 200 free texts. After 200, they cost $0.15 each.

 ii.  Plan B costs $20 a month, including 250 free texts. After 250, they cost $0.10 each.

*Monthly cost of Plan A:*  $A(t) = \begin{cases} 15, & if\ t \le 200 \\ 15 + 0.15(t - 200), & if\ t > 200 \end{cases}$   *where* $t$ *= number of texts per month*

*Monthly cost of Plan B:*  $B(t) = \begin{cases} 20, & if\ t \le 250 \\ 20 + 0.10(t - 250), & if\ t > 250 \end{cases}$   *where* $t$ *= number of texts per month*

## Problem Set Sample Solutions

If time allows, the following problem set can be used for additional practice. Otherwise, give this Problem Set as homework. Some of these questions will go one step further (i.e., they may ask an interpretive question), but they will not complete the modeling cycle.

1.  The costs to purchase school spirit posters are as follows: two posters for $5, four posters for $9, six posters for $13, eight posters for $17, and so on.

 a.  What type of function would best represent the cost of the total number of posters purchased?

 *Linear.*

 b.  What function represents the cost of the total number of posters purchased? How did you know? Justify your reasoning.

 *Let* $x$ *= number of school spirit posters. The four ordered pairs indicate a constant rate of change, (m = 2), so the equation will be* $y = 2x + b$. *To find b, we need to substitute any ordered pair, say* $(2, 5)$: $5 = 2(2) + b$, *so* $b = 1$. *The final equation for the function is* $f(x) = 2x + 1$.

 c.  If you have $40 to spend, write an inequality to find the maximum number of posters you could buy.

 $2x + 1 \le 40$

2.  NYC Sports Gym had 425 members in 2011. Based on statistics, the total number of memberships increases by 2% annually.

 a.  What type of function models the total number of memberships in this situation?

 *Exponential.*

 b.  If the trend continues, what function represents the total number of memberships in $n$ years? How did you know? Justify your reasoning.

 $f(n) = 425 (1 + 0.02)^n$

 *The initial number of members is 425. The yearly growth rate of 2% means I have to multiply by 1.02 for each year. So, 1.02 will be the common ratio for this exponential function.*

3. Derek hits a baseball thrown by the pitcher with an initial upward speed of 60 feet per second from a height of 3 feet.

a. What type of function models the height of the baseball versus time since it was hit?

*Quadratic.*

b. What is the function that models the height, $h$ (in feet), the baseball travels over a period of time in $t$ seconds? How did you know? Justify your reasoning.

*Since the initial velocity is 60 ft./second and the initial height is 3 ft., then I use the basic formula:*
$h(t) = -16t^2 + V_0 t + h_0$ *to find the function that describes the situation. The function equation is:*
$h(t) = -16t^2 + 60t + 3$

Lesson 3:    Analyzing a Verbal Description
Date:        10/4/13

# Mathematics Curriculum

Topic B:

# Completing the Modeling Cycle

**N-Q.A.2, N-Q.A.3, A-CED.A.1, A-CED.A.2, F-IF.B.4, F-IF.B.5, F-IF.B.6, F-BF.A.1a, F-LE.A.1b, F-LE.A.1c, F-LE.A.2**

| Focus Standard: | N-Q.A.2 | Define appropriate quantities for the purpose of descriptive modeling. |
|---|---|---|
| | N-Q.A.3 | Choose a level of accuracy appropriate to limitations on measurement when reporting quantities. |
| | A-CED.A.1 | Create equations and inequalities in one variable and use them to solve problems. *Include equations arising from linear and quadratic functions, and simple rational and exponential functions.*★ |
| | A-CED.A.2 | Create equations in two or more variables to represent relationships between quantities; graph equations on coordinate axes with labels and scales.★ |
| | F-IF.B.4 | For a function that models a relationship between two quantities, interpret key features of graphs and tables in terms of the quantities, and sketch graphs showing key features given a verbal description of the relationship. *Key features include: intercepts; intervals where the function is increasing, decreasing, positive, or negative; relative maximums and minimums; symmetries; end behavior; and periodicity.*★ |
| | F-IF.B.5 | Relate the domain of a function to its graph and, where applicable, to the quantitative relationship it describes. *For example, if the function h(n) gives the number of person-hours it takes to assemble n engines in a factory, then the positive integers would be an appropriate domain for the function.*★ |
| | F-IF.B.6 | Calculate and interpret the average rate of change of a function (presented symbolically or as a table) over a specified interval. Estimate the rate of change from a graph. |
| | F-BF.A.1a | Write a function that describes a relationship between two quantities.★ |
| | | a.   Determine an explicit expression, a recursive process, or steps for calculation from a context. |

| F-LE.A.1b F-LE.A.1c | Distinguish between situations that can be modeled with linear functions and with exponential functions.★ |
| | b.   Recognize situations in which one quantity changes at a constant rate per unit interval relative to another. |
| | c.   Recognize situations in which a quantity grows or decays by a constant percent rate per unit interval relative to another. |
| F-LE.A.2 | Construct linear and exponential functions, including arithmetic and geometric sequences, given a graph, a description of a relationship, or two input-output pairs (include reading these from a table).★ |

| **Instructional Days:** | 6 |
| **Lesson 4:** | Modeling a Context from a Graph |
| **Lesson 5:** | Modeling from a Sequence |
| **Lessons 6–7:** | Modeling a Context from Data |
| **Lessons 8–9:** | Modeling a Context from a Verbal Description |

Topic B follows a similar progression as Topic A, in that students create models for contexts presented as graphs, data, and as a verbal description. However, in this topic students complete the entire modeling cycle, from problem posing and formulation to validation and reporting. In Lesson 4, students use the gamut of functions covered in the Algebra I course for modeling purposes. They interpret the functions from their respective graphs: linear, quadratic, exponential, cubic, square root, cube root, absolute value, and other piecewise functions, including a return to some graphs from Topic A. Students build on their work from those lessons to complete the modeling cycle. Additionally, students will determine appropriate levels of numerical accuracy when reporting results.

Building on the work done with sequences in Topic A, in Lesson 5 students learn to recognize when a table of values represents an arithmetic (linear), geometric sequence (exponential), or quadratic sequence. In this lesson, patterns are presented as a table of values. Sequences that are neither arithmetic (linear) nor geometric (exponential) may also be explored (e.g., the product of two consecutive numbers: $a_n = n(n + 1)$).

In Lessons 6 and 7, students develop models from a given data set. They choose the appropriate function type, interpret key features of the function in context, and make predictions about future results based on their models. Some data sets will be recognized from Lesson 2 and from Module 2. Some will require a regression formula and/or a graphing calculator to compare correlation coefficients to find the best fit of the different function types.

Lessons 8 and 9 are the final lessons of the module and represent the culmination of much of the work students have done in the course. Here, contexts are presented as verbal descriptions from which students decide the type(s) of model to use: graphs, tables, or equations. They interpret the problems and create a function, table of values, and/or a graph to model the contextual situation described verbally, including those involving linear, quadratic, and exponential functions. They use graphs to interpret the function represented by the equation in terms of its context and answer questions about the model using the appropriate level of precision in reporting results. They interpret key features of the function and its graph and use both to answer questions related to the context, including calculating and interpreting the rate of change over an interval. When possible, students should articulate the shortcomings of the models they create; they should recognize what a model does and does not take into account.

# Lesson 4: Modeling a Context from a Graph

## Student Outcomes

- Students create a two-variable equation that models the graph from a context. Function types include linear, quadratic, exponential, square root, cube root, and absolute value. They interpret the graph and function and answer questions related to the model, choosing an appropriate level of precision in reporting their results.

## Lesson Notes

In Lesson 1 of Module 5, students practiced formulating a function from a graph, making it through the first two steps in the modeling cycle: *interpreting* a problem situation, and *formulating* a model. This lesson continues the modeling cycle by having students *compute, interpret,* and *validate*. This is an exploratory lesson, allowing students to practice modeling through prompts, and then discuss process with the class. The lesson ends with a difficult modeling exercise dealing with a square root function.

Refer to the modeling cycle below when abstracting and contextualizing (see pg. 61 of the CCLS and pg. 72 of the CCSS).

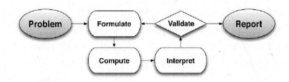

**Standards for Mathematical Practice:** Throughout this lesson, students work through the steps in the full modeling cycle. When presented with a problem they will make sense of the given information, analyze the presentation, define the variables involved, look for entry points to a solution, and create an equation to be used as a model. After formulating a model they perform computations, interpret the model, validate their results, make adjustments to the model when needed, and report results.

## Classwork

### Opening (10 minutes)

(Print and cut out the cards below before class begins. A card should have either a graph or a function, not both. Once the students are seated, hand out only one card to each student. Make sure to shuffle the cards so that the matches are not sitting right together. There are 34 cards altogether, 17 with graphs, and 17 with functions in equation form. Be sure to count ahead of time so that every function card has a matching graph. If there are an odd number of students, then you will need to take a card and play the matching game, as well. Instruct students to look at their cards and decide what the graph/function will look like for their match. Then have them hold up their cards so others can see it, and move around the room to look for their match. When the matches have found each other, have them stand next to each other. Check to make sure each pair is accurate before students return to their seats. [Note: This activity requires some estimation of values on the graph.]

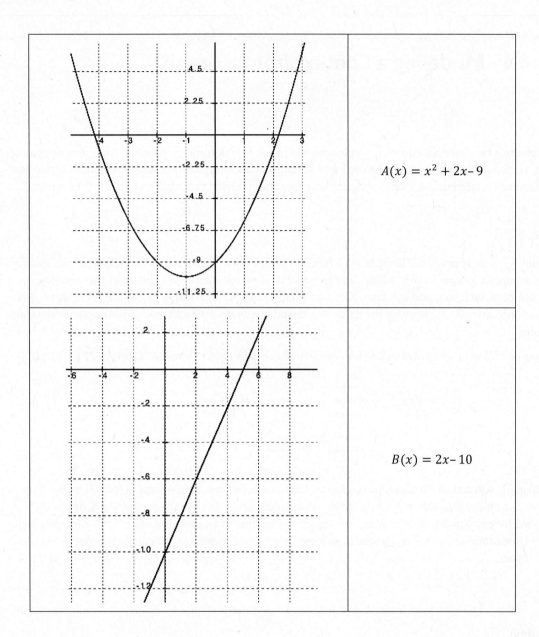

$A(x) = x^2 + 2x - 9$

$B(x) = 2x - 10$

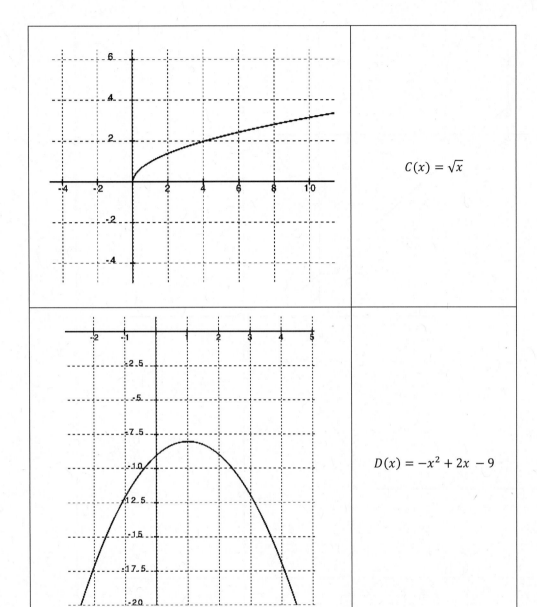

$C(x) = \sqrt{x}$

$D(x) = -x^2 + 2x - 9$

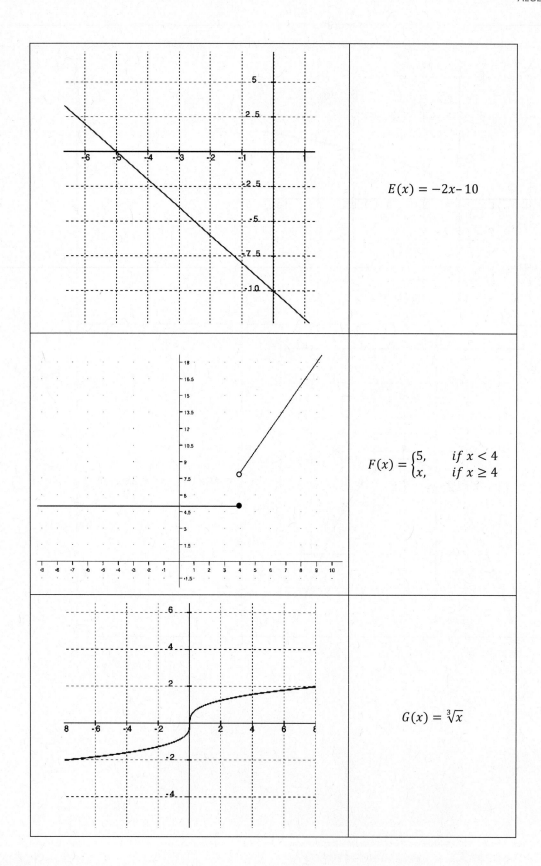

$E(x) = -2x - 10$

$F(x) = \begin{cases} 5, & \text{if } x < 4 \\ x, & \text{if } x \geq 4 \end{cases}$

$G(x) = \sqrt[3]{x}$

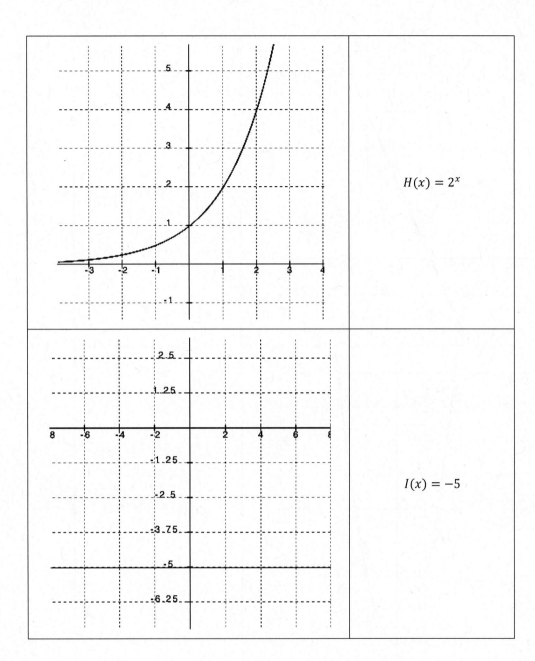

$H(x) = 2^x$

$I(x) = -5$

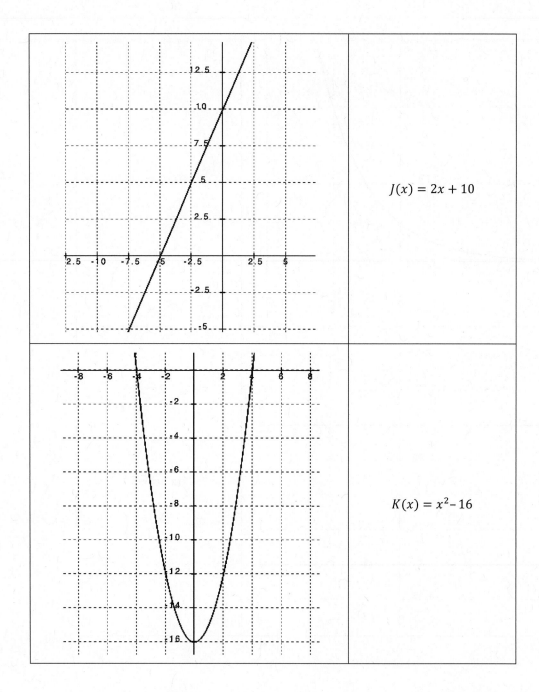

$J(x) = 2x + 10$

$K(x) = x^2 - 16$

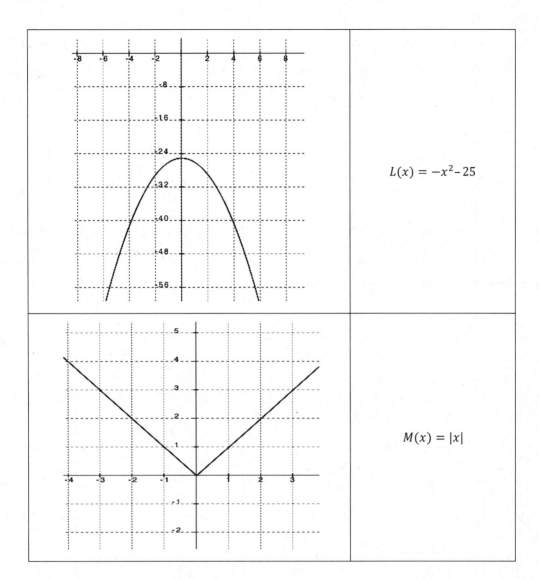

$$L(x) = -x^2 - 25$$

$$M(x) = |x|$$

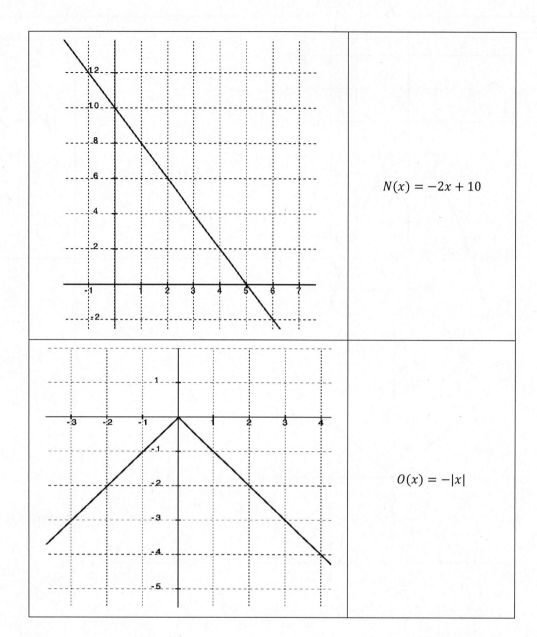

$N(x) = -2x + 10$

$O(x) = -|x|$

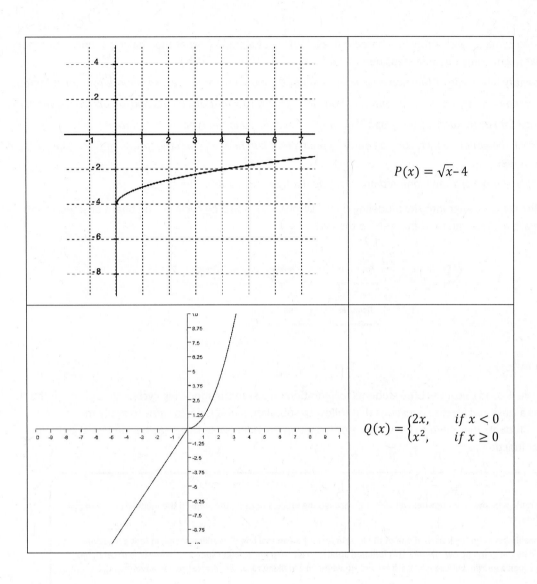

$$P(x) = \sqrt{x} - 4$$

$$Q(x) = \begin{cases} 2x, & \text{if } x < 0 \\ x^2, & \text{if } x \geq 0 \end{cases}$$

## Discussion (5 minutes)

- What was your strategy when trying to find your graph or function match?

  - *For the graph: I looked at the overall shape first to identify what type of graph it was (quadratic, linear, exponential, piecewise, square or cube root). I looked at end-behavior of the graph to determine the sign of the slope (linear) or leading coefficient (quadratic). I also looked at the x- and y-intercepts, domain, range, and any minimum or maximum y-values. Then, I looked for an equation to match these characteristics.*

  - *For the equation: I first looked for the function type, which narrowed my search considerably. Then, I looked for key features that are evident from the equation like: transformations, x- and/or y-intercepts, end behavior, slope, etc. Then, I looked for a graph with those characteristics.*

- If you had to come up with a function based only on looking at a graph (rather than having a function to match it to), what might some possible steps be?

  □ *Identify what type of function it is: linear, quadratic, exponential, piecewise, square root, or cube root.*

  □ *Compare the graph to the parent function: look for transformations (shifts and/or stretching/shrinking).*

  □ *Look for key features of the graph that may be recognized in the function's equation.*

  □ *Check the equation by testing a couple of points that can be read from the graph, or from a given table of values.*

  □ *Make a table of known ordered pairs to help analyze the values in the graph.*

The next activity will take us further into the modeling cycle. Display the modeling cycle on the board or screen and point out the parts of the activity that relate to the steps in the cycle.

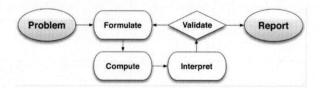

### Example 1 (10 minutes)

The following example is used to connect the students' exploration results to the modeling cycle. Work through the problem together as a class and use the questions that follow to stimulate a discussion of how to apply the steps in the full modeling cycle. Students may need to have the parent function provided since they may be somewhat unfamiliar with the square root function.

---

**Example 1**

**Read the problem below. Your teacher will walk you through the process of using the steps in the modeling cycle to guide in your solution:**

The relationship between the length of one of the legs, in feet, of an animal and its walking speed, in feet per second, can be modeled by the graph below. [Note: This function applies to *walking* not *running* speed. Obviously, a cheetah has shorter legs than a giraffe, but can run much faster. However, in a walking race, the giraffe has the advantage.]

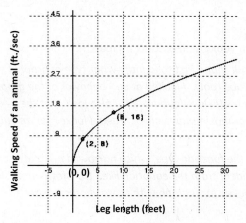

A T-Rex's leg length was 20 ft. What was the T-Rex's speed in ft./sec.?

---

- What are the units involved in this problem?  Define the quantities and variables you would use to model this graph.
  - *Leg length is in feet and speed is measured in feet per second, so time is measured in seconds.  Use x for the number of feet in leg length and $f(x)$ to represent the speed based on leg length.*

- What type of function does this graph represent?  What clues in the graph helped you recognize the function?
  - *There are only positive values and it starts at $(0,0)$, so this is probably a square root function, but it could be the right half of a cube root function.  I need to check a few points to be sure.*

After you get the correct response to the first question, draw or project the following three transformations of the square root function on the board or screen:  $f(x) = \sqrt{x}$, $g(x) = \sqrt{ax}$, $h(x) = \sqrt{(x-b)}$

- Which transformation of the function does this graph represent?  How can we determine that?
  - *Sample Response:  $f(x)$ cannot be the form because the square root of 2 is not 8, so it is either $g(x)$ or $h(x)$.  We can test both forms by substituting the x- and y-values from the points provided to us.*

    *First, check the form:  $g(x) = \sqrt{ax}$.*
    $$(2,8) \rightarrow 8 = \sqrt{2a} \rightarrow 64 = 2a \rightarrow a = 32$$
    $$(8,16) \rightarrow 16 = \sqrt{8a} \rightarrow 256 = 8a \rightarrow a = 32$$
    *Since we got $a = 32$ for both ordered pairs, it appears that $g(x)$ is the correct form and that $g(x) = \sqrt{32x}$.*

    *To make sure, we will also check the form:  $h(x) = \sqrt{(x-b)}$.*
    $$(2,8) \rightarrow 8 = \sqrt{(2-a)} \rightarrow 8^2 = 2 - b \rightarrow 64 = 2 - b \rightarrow b = -62$$
    $$(8,16) \rightarrow 16 = \sqrt{(8-b)} \rightarrow 16^2 = 8 - b \rightarrow 256 = 8 - b \rightarrow b = -248$$
    *The function cannot be $h(x)$.*

- Is the problem solved?
  - *We aren't finished.  Now we need to use the function we found to calculate the speed of the T-Rex with a 20-foot leg using $g(x) = \sqrt{32x}$.*
- What is the walking speed of the T-Rex?
  - $g(20) = \sqrt{(32)(20)} \rightarrow g(20) = \sqrt{640} \rightarrow g(20) = 8\sqrt{10}$, *or about 25 feet per second.*
- What if we doubled the length of T-Rex's legs, would the T-Rex walk twice as fast?
  - *A square root function does not double if the input is doubled.  The graph shows that when the input went from 2 to 8 the output does not quadruple.  A proportional relationship would have a double-the-input-double-the-output effect but a square root function is not proportional, a proportional relationship between two quantities must be linear.  If we look at the Eduardo graph (Exercise 1), we can see a proportional relationship.*

**Exercises 1–2 (20 minutes)**

Have students work in pairs or small groups on the following three exercises. You may want to do the first one as a guided exercise, depending on the needs of your students.

Remind the students that they saw Eduardo's work graph (shown below) in Lesson 1. At that time, we only formulated a model that could be used for that context. Now, we will further examine this context.

---

**Exercises**

Now practice using the modeling cycle with these problems:

1.  Eduardo has a summer job that pays him a certain rate for the first 40 hours per week and time and a half for any overtime. The graph below is a representation of how much money he earns as a function of the hours he works in one week.

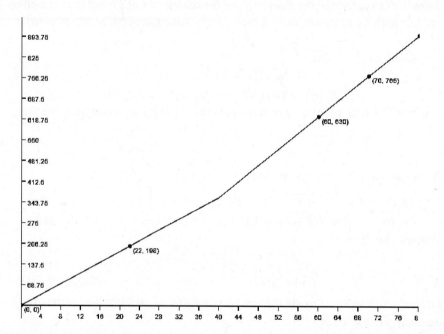

Eduardo's employers want to make him a salaried employee, which means he does not get overtime. If they want to pay him 480 dollars a week but have him commit to 50 hours a week, should he agree to the salary change? Justify your answer mathematically.

a.  *FORMULATE*  (recall this step from Lesson 1).

  i.  What type of function can be represented by a graph like this (e.g., quadratic, linear, exponential, piecewise, square root, or cube root)?

  *The graph is of a function that is piecewise defined and made up of two linear functions.*

  ii.  How would you describe the end-behavior of the graph in the context of this problem?

  *As x gets infinitely large, so does the function. However, realistically there is a limit to how many hours per week he can work, so there is a maximum value for this function.*

  iii.  How does this affect the equation of our function?

  *The slope for both graphs is positive. We may need to state restrictions on the domain, and also on the range.*

---

**b. COMPUTE**

**i.** What strategy do you plan to use to come up with the model for this context?

*Identify the domains for each piece (linear function) in the piecewise function. Find the slope and y-intercept for each linear piece, then put the equations in slope-intercept form.*

**ii.** Find the function of this graph. Show all your work.

*For the lower piece, domain: $0 \leq x \leq 40$.*
*The y-intercept is 0, and the given points in that domain that are $(0, 0)$ and $(22, 198)$. To calculate the slope $\frac{198}{22} = 9$.*
$f(x) = 9x \qquad if\ 0 \leq x \leq 40$

*For the upper piece, domain: $40 < x$.*
*This part of the problem requires using not only the graph, but also the context from the problem. Up to this point, Eduardo has worked 40 hours and has earned 9 dollars an hour. $40 \cdot 9 = 360$. This is his initial amount of earned money, or the y-intercept for the second linear equation. Again, we find the slope of the equation by selecting two points $(70, 765)$ and $(60, 630)$. $\frac{765-630}{70-60} = \frac{135}{10} = 13.50$.*

*Looking at the graph, we also see that the second line was moved 40 units to the right (translated), so x is $(x-40)$.*
$f(x) = 13.5(x-40) + 360 \quad if\ x > 40$

$$f(x) = \begin{cases} 9x, & if\ 0 \leq x \leq 40 \\ 13.5x + 360, & if\ x > 40 \end{cases}$$

**c. INTERPRET**

**i.** How much does Eduardo make an hour?

*$9 if $0 < x \leq 40$ and $13.50 if $x > 40$.*

**ii.** By looking only at the graphs, which interval has a greater average rate of change: $x < 20$, or $x > 45$? Justify your answer by making connections to the graph and its verbal description.

*The verbal description states that the Eduardo gets paid more after 40 hours of work. If you look at how the steep the graph is after 45 hours, you can see that it is increasing at a faster rate than when it was 20 hours or less.*

**iii.** Eduardo's employers want to make Eduardo a salaried employee, which means he does not get overtime. If they want to pay him 480 dollars a week but have him commit to 50 hours a week, should he agree to the salary change? Justify your answer mathematically.

*$f(50) = 13.5(50 - 40) + 360 \rightarrow 13.5(10) + 360 = 135 + 360 = $495$. He would get paid more as an hourly employee if he worked 50 hours a week. It seems that it would be in his best interest to keep the hourly agreement rather than the salary. Students may come up with other responses, but should at least understand that Eduardo earns more money for 50 hours of work as an hourly employee, than he would as a salaried employee. If students show that understanding, then they have answered the question correctly.*

**d. VALIDATE**

**i.** How can you check to make sure your function models the graph accurately?

*For the values in our graph, we can substitute the x-values into the function to see if the same given y-value is a result.*

Display this graph on the screen or board and use the questions that follow to explore the modeling cycle.

---

**2.** The cross-section view of a deep river gorge is modeled by the graph shown below where both height and distance are measured in miles. How long is a bridge that spans the gorge from the point labeled $(1, 0)$ to the other side? How high above the bottom of the gorge is the bridge?

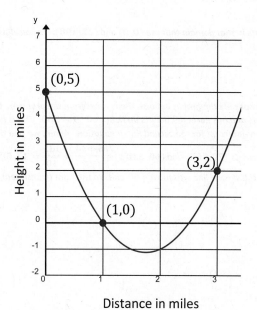

Distance in miles

a. **FORMULATE**

    i. What type of function can be represented by a graph like this? (Linear, quadratic, exponential, piecewise, square root, or cube root)

    *Quadratic.*

    ii. What are the quantities in this problem?

    *The quantities are height $f(x)$ relative to the location of the bridge and horizontal distance from the point highest point in the gorge $(x)$.*

    iii. How would you describe the end-behavior of the graph?

    *Opening upward.*

    iv. What is a general form for this function type?

    $f(x) = ax^2 + bx + c$ *or* $f(x) = a(x - h)^2 + k$ *or* $f(x) = a(x - m)(x - n)$

    v. How does knowing the function type and end-behavior affect the equation of the function for this graph?

    *The equation is a second-degree polynomial where the leading coefficient is positive.*

---

vi.  **What is the equation we would use to model this graph?**

*Using the three ordered pairs in the graph:*

$(0, 5)$: *From this pair, we see that* $c = 5$ *and* $f(x) = ax^2 + bx + 5$

*Now substitute the other two pairs to form a linear system:*

$(1, 0)$: $a + b = -5 \Rightarrow -3a - 3b = 15$

$(3, 2)$: $9a + 3b = -3$

*From here we see that* $6a = 12$ *and* $a = 2$. *So, substituting into the first linear equation, we have* $b = -7$

*So, the equation is* $f(x) = 2x^2 - 7x + 5$.

b.  <u>COMPUTE</u>

i.  **What are the key features of the graph that can be used to determine the equation?**

*The vertical intercept and the other two given ordered pairs.*

ii.  **Which key features of the function must be determined?**

*The zeros and the vertex must be determined.*

iii.  **Calculate the missing key features and check for accuracy with your graph.**

$f(x) = 2x^2 - 7x + 5$

*Using the sum-product property, we find:* $f(x) = (2x - 5)(x - 1)$. *So, the other end of the bridge is at the point* $(2.5, 0)$. *The vertex is located midway between the x-intercepts. Therefore,* $x = 1.75$. $f(1.75) = -1.125$.

c.  <u>INTERPRET</u>

i.  **What domain makes sense for this context?  Explain.**

*Since* $x$ *is the horizontal distance from* $(0, 5)$, *the domain that makes sense is* $x > 0$. *In order to know the upper limits of the domain, we would need to know the height of the highest point on the other side of the gorge, which cannot be determined with much accuracy from the given graph. We could assume it is between 3 and 3.5 miles.*

ii.  **How wide is the bridge with one side located at** $(1, 0)$**?**

*It would be the difference between the x-coordinates of the x-intercepts.* $2.5 - 1 = 1.5$ *miles wide.*

iii.  **How high is the bridge above the bottom of the gorge?**

*The minimum value of the function will represent the lowest point. Since the height shown on the graph is relative to the location of the bridge, the bridge would be* $1.125$ *miles above the bottom of the gorge. The y-coordinate of the minimum point represents that height below the bridge*

iv.  **Suppose the gorge is exactly** $3.5$ **feet wide from its two highest points. Find the average rate of change for the interval from** $x = 0$ **to** $x = 3.5$, $[0, 3.5]$**. Explain this phenomenon. Are there other intervals that will behave similarly?**

*The average rate of change for that interval is* $0$. *The two points are points of symmetry straight across the curve from each other. The line passing through them is horizontal. Any interval with endpoints that are symmetry points will be horizontal (0 slope).*

**d.   VALIDATE**

i.   How can you check to make sure that your function models the graph accurately?

*We can substitute any $x$-values from the graph into the function to see if the resulting $y$-value is reasonable for the graph.*

Now compare four representations that may be involved in the modeling process.   How is each useful for each phase of the modeling cycle?  Explain the advantages and disadvantages of each.

*The verbal description helps us define the quantities and, in this case, write the factored form of the equation for the function.  We always need to find another representation to analyze or interpret the situation.*

*The graph is visual and allows us to see the overall shape and end behavior of the function.  We can "see" some integer values of the function, but must estimate any non-integer values.  The graph is a good way to check calculations to make sure results are reasonable.*

*The table in general, does not help us to see shapes (patterns in $x - y$) any better than the graphs do.  However, a table with equal $x$-intervals does help us to see the patterns in $y$-values very well.*

*The equation allows us to accurately calculate values of the function for any real number.  It can be rewritten in various forms to help us see features of the function (vertex form, standard form, factored form).  It allows deep analysis and is sometimes referred to as an analytical model.*

## Closing (1 minute)

### Lesson Summary

When modeling from a graph use the full modeling cycle:

- FORMULATE – identify the variables involved, classify the type of graph presented, point out the visible key features, and create a different representation of the relationship if needed.

- COMPUTE – decontextualize the graph from the application and analyze it.  You might have to find symbolic or tabular representation of the graph to further analyze it.

- INTERPRET – contextualize the features of the function and your results and make sense of them in the context provided.

- VALIDATE – check your results with the context.  Do your answers make sense?  Are the calculations accurate?  Are there possibilities for error?

- REPORT – clearly write your results.

## Exit Ticket (2 minutes)

Lesson 4:     Modeling a Context from a Graph
Date:          10/4/13

66

Name _____    Date_____

# Lesson 4:  Modeling a Context from a Graph

**Exit Ticket**

1.  Why might we want to represent a graph of a function in analytical form?

2.  Why might we want to represent a graph as a table of values?

## Exit Ticket Sample Solutions

1.  **Why might we want to represent a graph of a function in analytical form?**

    *Graphs require estimation for many values, and for most we can calculate exact values using the function equation. Some key features that may not be visible or clear on a graph can be seen in the symbolic representation.*

2.  **Why might we want to represent a graph as a table of values?**

    *In a table of values, we can sometimes better see patterns in the relationship between the $x$- and $y$-values.*

## Problem Set Sample Solutions

Let the students know that these problems have little or no scaffolding and that they should use all the skills they learned in both Lessons 1 and 4 related to modeling a context from graphs.

1.  **During tryouts for the track team, Bob is running 90-foot wind sprints by running from a starting line to the far wall of the gym and back. At time, $t = 0$, he is at the starting line and ready to accelerate toward the opposite wall. As $t$ approaches 6 seconds he must slow down, stop for just an instant to touch the wall, then turn around, and sprint back to the starting line. His distance, in feet, from the starting line with respect to the number of seconds that has passed for one repetition, is modeled by the graph below.**

    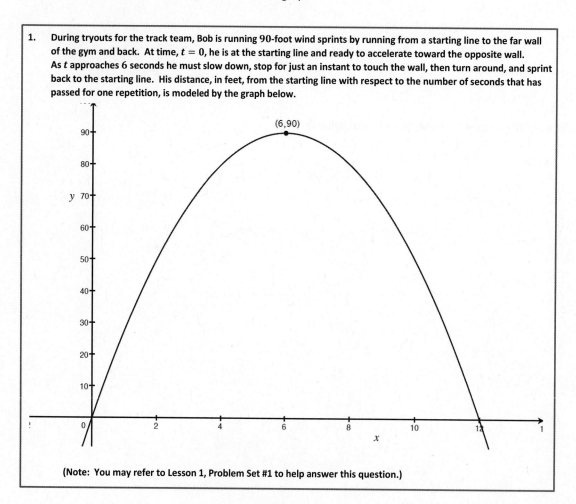

    (Note:  You may refer to Lesson 1, Problem Set #1 to help answer this question.)

How far was Bob from the starting line at 2 seconds? 6.5 seconds? (Distances, in meters, should be represented to the nearest tenth.)

*So far we know:*    $f(t) = a(t - 6)^2 + 90$ *[Now we need to find a.]*

*Substitute* $(0, 0)$:    $a(0 - 6)^2 + 90 = 0$

$a(-6)^2 + 90 = 0$

$36a = -90$

$a = \dfrac{-90}{36} = \dfrac{-15}{6}$

*The final function is:*    $f(x) = \dfrac{-15}{6}(t - 6)^2 + 90.$

*Now* $f(2)$:    $f(2) = \dfrac{-15}{6}(2 - 6)^2 + 90 = 50\ m$

*And* $f(6.5)$:    $f(6.5) = \dfrac{-15}{6}(6.5 - 6)^2 + 90 = 89.4\ m$

2.  Kyle and Abed each threw a baseball across a field. The height of the balls is described by functions $A(t)$ and $K(t)$, where $t$ is the number of seconds the baseball is in the air. $K(t)$ (equation below left) models the height of Kyle's baseball and $A(t)$ models the height of Abed's baseball (graph below):

$K(t) = -16t^2 + 66t + 6$

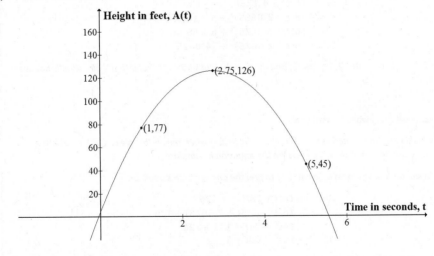

a.  Which ball was in the air for a longer period of time?

*We need to find the time when the ball is back on the ground (i.e., when the height function equals 0). First $A(t)$.*

*We can see from the graph that the ball is in the air from $t = 0$ to somewhere between 4 and 6. So, just by reading the graph, we might estimate the time in the air to be a little more than 5 seconds. We can get a more accurate number by formulating a model and then doing some calculations.*

*Using the vertex form:*    $A(t) = a(t - 2.75)^2 + 126$

*If we substitute (1, 77):*    $a(1 - 2.75)^2 + 126 = 77$

$3.0625a = -49$

$a = -49/3.0625 = -16$

| Lesson 4: | Modeling a Context from a Graph |
|-----------|--------------------------------|
| Date:     | 10/4/13                        |

69

*So:*                                $A(t) = -16(t - 2.75)^2 + 126 = 0$

*Now solve:*                         $-16(t - 2.75)^2 = -126$

$(t - 2.75)^2 = -126/-16$

$(t - 2.75)^2 = 7.875$

$t - 2.75 = \pm\sqrt{7.875}$

$t = 2.75 \pm \sqrt{7.875} = -0.06 \ or \ 5.6$

*Only the positive value makes sense in this context, so Abed's ball was in the air for 5.6 seconds.*

*Now for $K(t)$:*                    $K(t) = -16t^2 + 66t + 6$

*Using the quadratic formula to find the zeros:*

$t = \dfrac{-66 \pm \sqrt{66^2 - 4(-16)(6)}}{2(-16)} = \dfrac{-66 \pm \sqrt{4740}}{-32} \approx -0.09 \ or \ 4.2 \ seconds$

*Only the positive value makes sense in this context. So Kyle's ball was in the air for 4.2 seconds.*

*Abed's ball is in the air longer.*

b.   **Whose ball goes higher?**

*We see in the graph of $A(t)$ that the highest point for Abed's ball is 126 feet. Now we need to find the maximum value for $K(t)$. We will start by finding the vertex form for the equation:*

$$K(t) = -16(t^2 - 4.125t + \quad) + 6$$
$$= -16(t - 2.0625)^2 + 6 + 16(2.0625)^2$$
$$= -16(t - 2.0625)^2 + 6 + 68.0625$$
$$= -16(t - 2.0625)^2 + 74.0625$$

*So the vertex for $K(t)$ is $(2.0625, 74.0625)$ and Kyle's ball went about 74 feet into the air. Abed's ball went higher.*

c.   **How high was Abed's ball when he threw it?**

*Now we are looking for the y-intercept for $A(t)$ (i.e., the height when time is 0). We can either solve the vertex from equation for $t = 0$ or we can rewrite the equation in standard form.*

*Rewriting the equation is the most efficient way to find the answer to this question:*

$$A(t) = -16(t - 2.75)^2 + 126$$
$$= -16(t^2 - 5.5t + 7.5625) + 126$$
$$= -16t^2 - 88t - 121 + 126$$
$$A(t) = -16t^2 - 88t + 5$$

*That means (0, 5) is the vertical-intercept, and the ball was at 5 feet when thrown by Abed.*

*Or we can substitute $t = 0$ into the vertex form:*

$$A(t) = -16(t - 2.75)^2 + 126$$
$$= -16(0 - 2.75)^2 + 126$$
$$= -16(7.5625) + 126$$
$$= -121 + 126 = 5$$

*So the ball left Abed's hand at a height of 5 feet.*

# Lesson 5: Modeling from a Sequence

## Student Outcomes

- Students recognize when a table of values represents an arithmetic or geometric sequence. Patterns are present in tables of values. They choose and define the parameter values for a function that represents a sequence.

## Lesson Notes

This lesson will take students through the first steps of the modeling cycle, using functions that emerge from sequences. Refer to the modeling cycle below when abstracting and contextualizing. (See page 61 of the CCSS or page 72 of the CCSS.)

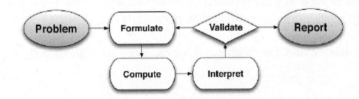

**Standards for Mathematical Practice:** Throughout the lesson students will look for and make use of structure. Students will look closely to discern a pattern or structure of a sequence of numbers and be able to determine if a sequence is arithmetic, geometric or neither. Students will also use the modeling cycle to solve problems that occur in everyday life.

## Classwork

Remind your students that in Module 3, Lessons 1, 2, and 3, they learned about the linear relationship in arithmetic sequences and the exponential relationship in geometric sequences. If your students could benefit from a review of sequences, use the review that follows. If they are ready to begin, then skip to the Opening on page 73. [Note: You may choose to use the subscript notation for the expressions/equations when dealing with sequences.]

*Scaffolding:*

Point out:  *A sequence* is a list of numbers or objects in a special order.  But first we are going to learn about *geometric and arithmetic sequences.*  There are two sequences in this problem.  Let's review how both types are defined using the following examples:

*Arithmetic Sequence* – An arithmetic sequence goes from one term to the next by adding (or subtracting) the same value.

(Note:  Be sure to pronounce *arithmetic* correctly.  In this case, it is used as an adjective and has the emphasis on the third syllable [*adj.* ar-ith-*met*-ik] rather than on the second, as students are used to hearing it.)

Example:  Start with 1, add 3 to find the next term:

| $n$ | 1 | 2 | 3 | 4 | 5 | 6 | ... | $n$ |
|---|---|---|---|---|---|---|---|---|
| $f(n)$ | 1 | 4 | 7 | 10 | 13 | 16 | | |
| | 1 | $1+3$ | $1+2(3)$ | $1+3(3)$ | $1+4(3)$ | $1+5(3)$ | | $1+(n-1)(3)$ |

$f(n) = 1 + 3(n-1) = 1 + 3n - 3 = 3n - 2$

Generally, we have: $f(n) = $ (starting number) $+ (n-1)$(common difference).

[Note:  This form is called the *explicit formula* and may also be written using subscripts: $a_n = 3n - 2$.]

For some sequences, it is appropriate to use a *recursive formula*, which defines the terms of the sequence based on the term before. In this case:  $f(n+1) = f(n) + 3$, $f(1) = 1$; *or using subscript notation:* $a_{n+1} = a_n + 3$

If we agree to call the initial value $A$ and the common difference $d$, we can write the expression more simply as:

$f(n) = A + (n-1)d$

- Can you see from the graph that the relationship between n and the corresponding number in the sequence is a line?  And that the slope of the line is 3?  How is that related to the way the sequence is expanded?

  □ *Yes, since $n$ is the list of consecutive counting numbers, we add 1 to find the next.  To find the next $f(n)$ value we add three.  Those two numbers, 3 and 1, are the rise and the run, respectively, for the points on the graph, and so will determine the slope of the line.*

*Geometric Sequence* – A geometric sequence goes from one term to the next by multiplying (or dividing) by the same value.

Example:  Start with 400, multiply by $\frac{1}{4}$ to find the next term:

| $n$ | 1 | 2 | 3 | 4 | ... | $n$ |
|---|---|---|---|---|---|---|
| $f(n)$ | 400 | 100 | 25 | 6.25 | | |
| | 400 | $400\left(\frac{1}{4}\right)1$ | $400\left(\frac{1}{4}\right)2$ | $400\left(\frac{1}{4}\right)3$ | | $400\left(\frac{1}{4}\right)^{(n-1)}$ |

We have 400 as the first term and every term after than is multiplied by $\frac{1}{4}$.

This makes the exponent one less than the term number.

For this sequence we have: $f(n) = 400\left(\frac{1}{4}\right)^{(n-1)}$

And in general terms, we have: $f(n) = (starting\ number)(common\ ratio)^{(n-1)}$

If we agree to call the initial value $A$, and the common ratio $r$, we can write the expression more simply as:

$$f(n) = Ar^{(n-1)}$$

- Do you see from the graph that the relationship between n and the corresponding number in the sequence is exponential?

## Opening (5 minutes)

Have students read the following problem and then, with a partner or small group, brainstorm the possible entry points to the solutions. Make sure they notice that there are two sequences involved, one for the length of time on each exercise, and one for the length of rest time. After they work for a while on the three questions, ask: "Why would sequences be appropriate to model this situation?" Hopefully, they will have discovered that the first column is arithmetic (linear), and the second is geometric (exponential). Also note that sequences are a good idea when the domain being modeled is whole numbers.

---

**Opening Exercise**

A soccer coach is getting her students ready for the season by introducing them to High Intensity Interval Training (HIIT). She presents the table below with a list of exercises for an HIIT training circuit and the length of time that must be spent on each exercise before the athlete gets a short time to rest. The rest times increase as the students complete more exercises in the circuit. Study the chart and answer the questions below. How long would the 10th exercise be? If a player had 30 minutes of actual gym time during a period, how many exercises could she get done? Explain your answers.

| Exercise # | Length of Exercise Time | Length of Rest Time |
|---|---|---|
| Exercise 1 | $0.5$ minute | $0.25$ minute |
| Exercise 2 | $0.75$ minute | $0.5$ minute |
| Exercise 3 | 1 minute | 1 minute |
| Exercise 4 | $1.25$ minutes | 2 minutes |
| Exercise 5 | $1.5$ minutes | 4 minutes |

---

## Discussion (15 minutes)

Display each of the two sequences from the opening separately, showing the relationship between the number of the term, $n$, and the term in the sequence. Have students discuss the relationships with a partner or small group. Then use the guiding questions to inspire the discussion. (Remind students that they have studied sequences in earlier modules.) Use the tables to show that the relationship is linear for the sequence that is found by adding a constant value (the common difference) to find the next term. And then show that the relationship is exponential for the sequence that is found by multiplying by a constant value (the common ratio) to find the next term.

- What are the quantities and variables we need to define to solve this problem?
    - *Units are minutes of exercise time and minutes of rest time. Since we have two different sequences and both are related to the number of the exercise, it is likely that students will let some variable, say, $n$, represent the exercise number and the other two columns be $E(n)$ and $R(n)$.*

- How can we tell what type of sequence represents the completion times for the exercises?
    - *We can check to see if there is a common difference by subtracting any two consecutive terms. If the difference is constant, then it is arithmetic.*

---

| Exercise | Exercise Time | Difference |
|----------|---------------|------------|
| Exercise 1 | 0.5 minute | |
| Exercise 2 | 0.75 minute | 0.25 |
| Exercise 3 | 1 minute | 0.25 |
| Exercise 4 | 1.25 minutes | 0.25 |
| Exercise 5 | 1.5 minutes | 0.25 |

- ▫ *In this case, the sequence representing completion time for an exercise is arithmetic so there is no need to look for a common ratio.*

- ■ How can we tell what type of sequence the rest time is?
  - ▫ *We can subtract each term in the sequence to see if the increase is by the same number. If it is, then the sequence is arithmetic. If it is not, then the sequence might be geometric but we would still need to make sure.*

| Exercise | Rest Time | Common Difference | Common Ratio |
|----------|-----------|-------------------|--------------|
| Exercise 1 | 0.25 minute | | |
| Exercise 2 | 0.5 minute | 0.25 | $\dfrac{0.5}{0.25} = 2$ |
| Exercise 3 | 1 minute | 0.5 | $\dfrac{1}{0.5} = 2$ |
| Exercise 4 | 2 minutes | 1 | $\dfrac{2}{1} = 2$ |
| Exercise 5 | 4 minutes | 2 | $\dfrac{4}{2} = 2$ |

- ■ It is not arithmetic but it could be geometric. We have to analyze the ratio by dividing one term by the previous term. Looking at the column to the far right we can see that the sequence for Rest Time is geometric.
- ■ What is the symbolic form of the two functions?
  - ▫ *Sample responses:*

    *Exercise time, $E$:*

    $E(n) = 0.5 + 0.25(n - 1)$ *where $n$ stands for exercise number, $n \geq 1$.*

    *Rest time, $R$:*

    $R(n) = (0.25)(2)^{(n-1)}$ *where $n$ stands for exercise number, $n \geq 1$.*

- Now let's look at those two questions below the original table. How long would the 10th exercise be?
  - *Sample response:* $E(10) = 0.5 + 0.25(10 - 1) = 2.75$ *minutes*
- If a student has up to 30 minutes of actual gym time during a soccer practice, how many exercises in the circuit would she be able to complete? Explain your answer.
  - *We would have to add the Exercise and Rest Times for each row starting with Exercise 1 and see when the cumulated time exceeds 30 minutes. Here are the numbers for Exercises 1 – 5:* $0.75 + 1.25 + 2 + 3.25 + 5.5 = 12.75$
  
    *If we continue the table, we can see that we then have to add:* $12.75 + 9.75 = 22.5$. *Then, for Exercise 7 we are up to more than 40 minutes.*

| Exercise | Exercise Time | Rest Time | Total Circuit Time |
|----------|---------------|-----------|--------------------|
| Exercise 5 | 1.5 minutes | 4 minutes | 12.75 |
| Exercise 6 | 1.75 minutes | 8 minutes | 22.5 |
| Exercise 7 | 2 minute | 16 minutes | 40.5 minutes |

  - *So, Exercise 6 can be completed (including rest/recovery times) in 22.5 minutes. There is just enough time to complete Exercise 7, for a total workout time of 38.5 minutes before the player heads to the locker room. [Note: Students may say that there is time to finish six exercises with the rest time to follow. This would be correct if we had to include the rest time at the end of the last exercise.]*

## Example 1 (5 minutes)

Write this sequence on the board or screen. Have students work with a partner or small group.

---

**Example 1**

Determine whether the sequence below is arithmetic or geometric, and to find the function that will produce any given term in the sequence:

$$16, 24, 36, 54, 81, \ldots$$

---

You might use this example as an independent or guided task, depending on the needs of your students.

---

**Is this sequence arithmetic?**

*The differences are 8, 12, 18, 27, … so right away we can tell this is not arithmetic – there is no common difference.*

**Is the sequence geometric?**

*The ratios are all* $1.5$, *so this is geometric.*

**What is the analytical representation of the sequence?**

*Since the first term is 16 and the common ratio is* $1.5$ *we have:* $f(n) = 16(1.5)^{n-1}$

---

## Exercises 1–3  (15 minutes)

Have students look at the sequence for each table, and then determine the analytical representation of the sequence. You might decide to use these exercises as independent practice, guided practice, or for small group work, depending on the needs of your students.  Try to move them toward independence as soon as possible.

---

**Exercises**

Look at the sequence and determine the analytical representation of the sequence.  Show your work and reasoning.

1.  A decorating consultant charges $50 for the first hour and $2 for each additional whole hour.  How much would 1000 hours of consultation cost?

| $n$ | 1 | 2 | 3 | 4 | 5 | ... | $n$ |
|---|---|---|---|---|---|---|---|
| $f(n)$ | 50 | 52 | 54 | 56 | 58 | | ? |

*By subtracting, we see that this is an arithmetic sequence where we are adding 2, but starting at 50.*

$$f(n) = 50 + 2n$$
$$f(1000) = 50 + 2000 = \$2050$$

2.  The sequence below represents the area of a square whose side length is the diagonal of a square with integer side length $n$. What would be the area for the 100$^{th}$ square?  [Hint:  You can use the square below to find the function model, but you can also just use the terms of the sequence.]

| $n$ | 1 | 2 | 3 | 4 | 5 | ... | $n$ |
|---|---|---|---|---|---|---|---|
| $f(n)$ | 2 | 8 | 18 | 32 | 50 | | ? |

*Looking at first differences, we see that they are not the same (no common difference):  6, 10, 14, 18, ....*

*When we look for a common ratio, we find that the quotients of any two consecutive terms in the sequence are not the same:  $8/2 \neq 18/8 \neq 32/18, ...$*

*However, I noticed that the first difference increases by 4.  This is an indication of a quadratic sequence and the function equation must have an $n^2$. But since for $n = 1$ we would have $n^2 = 1$, we must need to multiply that by 2 to get the first term. Now check to see if $2n^2$ will work for the other terms.*

$$f(n) = 2n^2$$

*Checking:*  $f(2) = 2(2^2) = 8$
$f(3) = 2(3^2) = 18$

*Yes! It works. So ...*

$f(100) = 2(100)^2 = 20,000.$  *So, the area of the 100$^{th}$ square is 20,000 square units.*

---

3. What would the 10th term in the sequence be?

| $n$ | 1 | 2 | 3 | 4 | ... | $n$ |
|---|---|---|---|---|---|---|
| $f(n)$ | 3 | 6 | 12 | 24 | | ? |

*There is no common difference. But the ratios are:* $\frac{6}{3} = 2$, $\frac{12}{6} = 2$, $\frac{24}{12} = 2$, .... *This is a geometric sequence with a common ratio of 2. And the terms are as follows:*

| $n$ | 1 | 2 | 3 | 4 | ... | 10 |
|---|---|---|---|---|---|---|
| $f(n)$ | 3 | 3(2) | 3(4) | 3(8) | | $3(2^9)$ |

*The 10th term in the sequence is* $3(512) = 1536$.

> **Suggestion:**
>
> Ask students who enjoy a challenge to see if they can find another way to define the $n^{th}$ term for Exercise 3. [They may discover that they can use $2^n$ in the expression if they change the number they multiply by to 1.5. Then, the function would be $f(n) = 1.5(2^n)$. Check it out.]

## Closing (1 minute)

> **Lesson Summary**
>
> - A sequence is a list of numbers or objects in a special order.
> - An arithmetic sequence goes from one term to the next by adding (or subtracting) the same value.
> - A geometric sequence goes from one term to the next by multiplying (or dividing) by the same value.
> - Looking at the difference of differences can be a quick way to determine if a sequence can be represented as a quadratic expression.

## Exit Ticket (4 minutes)

Name _____ Date_____

# Lesson 5: Modeling From a Sequence

Exit Ticket

1. A culture of bacteria doubles every 2 hours.

    a. Explain how this situation can be modeled with a sequence.

    b. If there are 500 bacteria at the beginning, how many bacteria will there be after 24 hours?

## Exit Ticket Sample Solutions

1. A culture of bacteria doubles every 2 hours.

   a. Explain how this situation can be modeled with a sequence.

      *To find the next number of bacteria, you multiply the previous number by 2. This situation can be represented by a geometric sequence. There will be a common ratio between each term of the sequence.*

   b. If there are 500 bacteria at the beginning, how many bacteria will there be after 24 hours?

      *Since the bacteria splits (reproduces) every two hours, then n represents 12 splits in the 24-hour period.*

      $f(n) = (initial\ amount)(common\ ratio)^{(n-1)}$. *Or, in terms of the context: the 500 bacteria cells will double 11 times in 24 hours.*

      $f(n) = 500(2)^{12-1} = 500(2)^{11} = 1,024,000\ bacteria.$

## Problem Set Sample Solutions

Solve the following problems by finding the function/formula that represents the $n^{th}$ term of the sequence.

1. After a knee injury, a jogger is told he can jog 10 minutes every day, and that he can increase his jogging time by 2 minutes every two weeks. How long will it take for him to be able to jog one hour a day?

   *This is an arithmetic sequence where the minutes increase by 2 every two weeks. [Note: We can either let 2n represent the number of weeks, or let n represent a 2-week period. Either way, we will end up having to compensate after we solve.] Let's try it with n representing a 2-week period:*

   $$f(n) = initial\ time + (n-1)(common\ difference)$$
   $$60 = 10 + (n-1)(2) \rightarrow 60 = 10 + 2n - 2 \rightarrow 60 = 2n + 8$$
   $$2n + 8 = 60 \rightarrow 2n = 52 \rightarrow n = 26$$
   *Since it's every two weeks, we need to multiply 26 by 2. So it takes 52 weeks (or 12 months) for the jogger to be able to jog for 60 minutes.*

| Week # | Daily Jog Time |
|--------|----------------|
| 1 | 10 |
| 2 | 10 |
| 3 | 12 |
| 4 | 12 |
| 5 | 14 |
| 6 | 14 |

2. A ball is dropped from a height of 10 feet. The ball then bounces to 80% of its previous height with each subsequent bounce.

   a. Explain how this situation can be modeled with a sequence.

      *According to the problem, to find the next height you multiply the current height by 0.8. This means the sequence is geometric.*

   b. How high (*to the nearest tenth of a foot*) does the ball bounce on the fifth bounce?

      $f(n) = (initial\ height)(common\ ratio)^n$ *for n bounces.*

      $f(5) = 10(0.8)^5 \approx 3.3$ *– to the nearest foot is 3 feet for 5 bounces.*

3. Consider the following sequence:

$$8, 17, 32, 53, 80, 113, \ldots$$

a. What pattern do you see, and what does that pattern mean for the analytical representation of the function?

*Difference of the difference is 6. Since the second difference is a non-zero constant, then the pattern must be quadratic.*

b. What is the symbolic representation of the sequence?

*Sample response: $3n^2$ does not work by itself (If $n = 1$, then $3n^2$ would be 3, but we have an 8 for the first term.) So, there must be a constant that is being added to it. Let's test that theory:*

$$f(n) = 3n^2 + b$$
$$f(1) = 3(1)^2 + b = 8$$
$$3 + b = 8$$
$$b = 5$$

*So, the terms of the sequence can be found using the number of the term, as follows:*

$$\underline{f(n) = 3n^2 + 5}$$

*We can easily check to see if this function generates the sequence, and it does.*

4. Arnold wants to be able to complete 100 military-style pull-ups. His trainer puts him on a workout regimen designed to improve his pull-up strength. The following chart shows how many pull-ups Arnold can complete after each month of training. How many months will it take Arnold to achieve his goal if this pattern continues?

*This pattern does not have a common difference or a common ratio. When we look at the first differences $(3, 5, 7, 9, 11, \ldots)$, we see that the second differences would be constant $(2, 2, 2, \ldots)$. That means this is a quadratic sequence with $n^2$ in the $n^{th}$ term formula. For $n = 1$ we have $1^2 = 1$ so we need to add 1 to get the first term to be 2. So, in general, we have:*

*$f(n) = n^2 + 1$. Let's test that on the other terms: $2^2 + 1 = 5, 3^2 + 1 = 10, \ldots$ Yes, it works.*

*Now we need to find out which month ($n$) will produce 100 as the resulting number of pull-ups:*

$$n^2 + 1 = 100 \rightarrow n = \sqrt{99} \approx 9.9$$

*So, if this trend continues, at $\underline{10\ months}$ Arnold will be able to complete 100 pull-ups.*

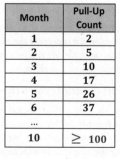

| Month | Pull-Up Count |
|-------|---------------|
| 1 | 2 |
| 2 | 5 |
| 3 | 10 |
| 4 | 17 |
| 5 | 26 |
| 6 | 37 |
| ... | |
| 10 | $\geq 100$ |

# Lesson 6: Modeling a Context from Data

## Student Outcomes

- Students write equations to model data from tables, which can be represented with linear, quadratic, or exponential functions, including several from Lessons 4 and 5. They recognize when a set of data can be modeled with a linear, exponential, or quadratic function and create the equation that models the data.
- Students interpret the function in terms of the context in which it is presented, make predictions based on the model, and use an appropriate level of precision for reporting results and solutions.

## Lesson Notes

This real-life descriptive modeling lesson is about creating different types of functions based on data, including linear, quadratic, and exponential. This lesson uses the full modeling cycle as explained on page 61 of the CCLS or page 72 of the CCSS.

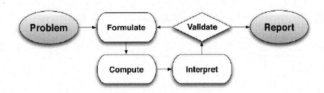

(Note: This lesson will likely require a calculator and graph paper.)

## Classwork

### Opening (5 minutes)

Display the three sets of data below on the board or screen. Divide the class up into three sections. Each section has to analyze one table. Students must complete the following:

---

**Opening Exercise**

1. Identify the type of function the each table represents (e.g., quadratic, linear, exponential, square root, etc.).

2. Explain how you were able to identify the function.

3. Find the symbolic representation of the function.

4. Plot the graphs of your data.

**A**

| x | y |
|---|----|
| 1 | 5 |
| 2 | 7 |
| 3 | 9 |
| 4 | 11 |
| 5 | 13 |

**B**

| x | y |
|---|--------|
| 1 | 6 |
| 2 | 9 |
| 3 | 13.5 |
| 4 | 20.25 |
| 5 | 30.375 |

**C**

| x | y |
|---|----|
| 1 | 3 |
| 2 | 12 |
| 3 | 27 |
| 4 | 48 |
| 5 | 75 |

---

Have one student from each section share the work of his or her group with the class and explain the group's approach. Discuss the strategies of each group. Make sure all students are grounded in the three procedures for recognizing the three basic functions (i.e., linear, quadratic, and exponential).

*Scaffolding:*

Have students create a "crib sheet" for the three different functions (i.e., linear, exponential and quadratic), with information for how to identify them and completed examples. This might be part of their journals/notebooks for this module.

1. **A: linear**      **B: Exponential**      **C: Quadratic**

2. *I see that the difference of each output for:*
   *A: is constant so that it is linear (common difference is 2),*
   *B: is a geometric sequence (common ratio is 1.5), and for*
   *C: if I found the difference of the differences is the same number (6), so it is quadratic.*

3. A: $f(x) = 2x + 3$      B: $f(x) = 4(1.5^x)$      C: $f(x) = 3x^2$

4.

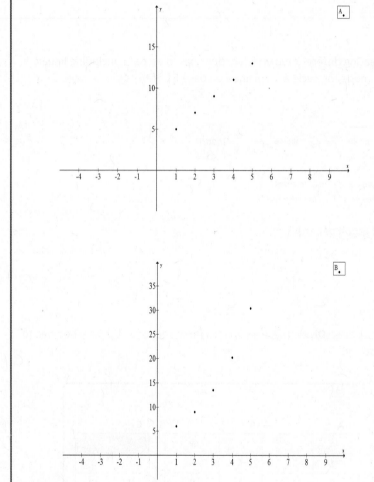

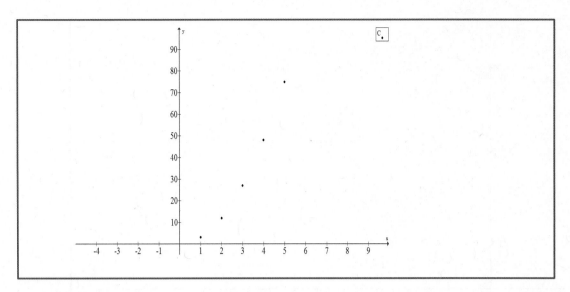

## Example 1 (15 minutes)

- Point out: The approach we take when examining sequences and tables can be used when we want to model data.

Present the following problem and have students work with a partner or small group to answer the questions related to the data set. Depending on the needs of your students, you might use this example as an independent exercise, or a guided group activity. Some scaffolding suggestions are offered in the box on the right that you might use to get the students started on building the model. [Note: This example is designed to be a quadratic pattern that appears linear, with no accounting for statistical variability in measurement.]

*Scaffolding:*

You might begin with this example as a guided activity to help struggling students get started. Then let them try to create and use student responses to guide the discussion further, if needed.

- Start by plotting the pairs in the table using the values in the second and third columns.
- Let's look at the graph of this data (see below). (Window $-x$: $[0,5]$, $y$: $[450, 1000]$)
- The graph appears to be linear, but it's important to remember the window we are looking at might be hiding some important features of the graph. Try changing the window to see what is happening in other parts of the coordinate plane.
- This could be a quadratic graph. We will need to investigate further with the data.
- So, let's look for common differences and key features in the table.

**Example 1**

Enrique is a biologist who has been monitoring the population of a rare fish in Lake Placid. He has tracked the population for 5 years, and has come up with the following estimates:

| Year Tracked | Year since 2002 | Estimated Fish Population |
|---|---|---|
| 2002 | 0 | 1000 |
| 2003 | 1 | 899 |
| 2004 | 2 | 796 |
| 2005 | 3 | 691 |
| 2006 | 4 | 584 |

Create a graph and a function to model this situation and use it to predict (assuming the trend continues) when the fish population will be gone from the Lake Placid ecosystem. Verify your results, and explain the limitations of each model.

*When we plot this data in a reasonable viewing window, the data appears to be linear. The limitations to using a graph are that it is difficult to get a viewing window that allows us to see all of the key features of the function represented. When we look at the first differences, we can see that this is not a linear relationship. To determine when the fish population will be gone, we need to find the function to model this situation.*

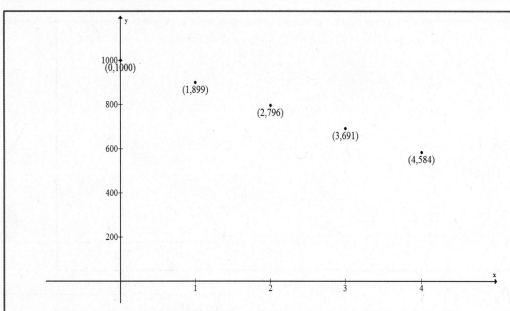

*Looking at differences may help us identify the function type. The first differences are $101, 103, 105, 107$, etc. These are not the same, but are at regular intervals. That tells us that there will be a common second difference, in this case 2. This data can be modeled with a quadratic function.*

*Creating a symbolic representation:*

*The standard form for a quadratic function is:*

$$f(x) = ax^2 + bx + c$$

*We know that $(0, 1000)$ is the y-intercept. That tells us $c = 1000$. Now we have:*

$$f(x) = ax^2 + bx + 1000$$

*Substitute $(1, 899)$:*     $899 = a + b + 1000 \rightarrow a + b = -101$

*Substitute $(2, 796)$:*     $796 = 4a + 2b + 1000 \rightarrow 4a + 2b = -204$

*Now solve the linear system:*

$$\begin{array}{r} 202 = -2a - 2b \\ -204 = \phantom{-}4a + 2b \\ \hline -2 = \phantom{-}2a \phantom{+2b} \rightarrow a = -1 \end{array}$$

*Now solve for b:*     $-1 + b = -101$     $\rightarrow b = -100$

*The function model is:*     $\underline{f(x) = -x^2 - 100x + 1000}$

*So, now we need to determine when the fish population will be 0.*

*Solve:*     $0 = -x^2 + 100x + 1000$

*Using the quadratic formula:*  $x = \dfrac{100 \pm \sqrt{(-100)^2 - 4(-1)(1000)}}{2(-1)} \approx -109.16 \text{ or } 9.16$

*Since only the positive number of years is reasonable in this situation, we will say that $x = 9.16$ years after 2002.*

*Depending on whether the initial measurement is taken at the beginning of 2002 or at the end, we could say that the fish population will be gone during 2011, or that it will be gone by 2012.*

*The function model has fewer limitations than the graph, but it provides results that need to be interpreted in the context of the problem.*

**Lesson 6:**    Modeling a Context from Data
**Date:**       10/4/13

84

**Standards for Mathematical Practice:** This problem requires that students make decisions about precision during their problem solving process but especially at the end when they must answer the question about which year the fish population will actually be gone.

Students may decide to extend the table. Here is what they will find. Make sure that they also create the function, verify their results, and discuss the limitations of their model.

| Year Tracked | Year since 2002 | Estimated Fish Population | 1st Difference | 2nd Difference |
|---|---|---|---|---|
| 2002 | 0 | 1000 | 0 | |
| 2003 | 1 | 899 | 101 | 2 |
| 2004 | 2 | 796 | 103 | 2 |
| 2005 | 3 | 691 | 105 | 2 |
| 2006 | 4 | 584 | 107 | 2 |
| 2007 | 5 | 475 | 109 | 2 |
| 2008 | 6 | 364 | 111 | 2 |
| 2009 | 7 | 251 | 113 | 2 |
| 2010 | 8 | 136 | 115 | 2 |
| 2011 | 9 | 19 | 117 | 2 |
| 2012 | 10 | *Fish are gone* | | |

## Exercises 1–3 (20 minutes)

**Exercises**

1.  Bella is a BMX bike racer and wants to identify the relationship between her bike's weight and the height of jumps (a category she gets judged on when racing). On a practice course, she tests out 7 bike models with different weights and comes up with the following data.

    | Weight (lbs.) | Height (ft.) |
    |---|---|
    | 20 | 8.9 |
    | 21 | 8.82 |
    | 22 | 8.74 |
    | 23 | 8.66 |
    | 24 | 8.58 |
    | 25 | 8.5 |
    | 26 | 8.42 |
    | 27 | 8.34 |

    a.  Bella is sponsored by Twilight Bikes and must ride a 32-lb bike. What can she expect her jump height to be?

    *By looking at the differences between the terms, we can identify that this is a linear relationship (or an arithmetic sequence) that decreases by $0.08$ for every 1-lb increase in weight.*

    $$8.9 = a_1 - 0.08(20) \rightarrow 8.9 = a_1 - 1.6 \rightarrow a_1 = 10.5$$

    $$h(w) = 10.5 - 0.08w$$

    $$h(32) = 10.5 - 0.08(32) = 7.94 \, ft.$$

b.  Bella asks the bike engineers at Twilight to make the lightest bike possible. They tell her the lightest functional bike they could make is 10 lb. Based on this data, what is the highest she should expect to jump if she only uses Twilight bikes?

$$h(w) = 10.5 - 0.08w$$

$$h(10) = 10.5 - 0.08(10) = 9.7 \, ft.$$

c.  What is the maximum weight of a bike if Bella's jumps have to be at least 2 feet high during a race?

$$h(w) = 10.5 - 0.08w$$

$$2 = 10.5 - 0.08(w) \rightarrow w = 106.25 \, lbs.$$

2.  The concentration of medicine in a patient's blood as time passes is recorded in the table below.

| Time (hours) | Concentration of Medicine (ml) |
|:---:|:---:|
| 0 | 0 |
| 0.5 | 55.5 |
| 1 | 83 |
| 1.5 | 82.5 |
| 2 | 54 |

a.  The patient cannot be active while the medicine is in his blood. How long, to the nearest minute, must the patient remain inactive? What are the limitations of your model(s)?

*If we plot the points, we can see a general shape for the graph.*

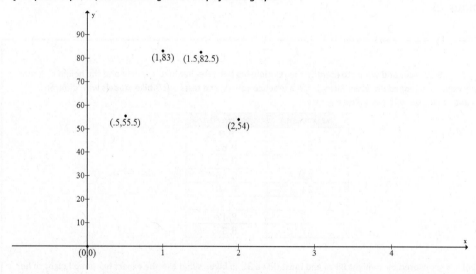

*This might be a quadratic relationship, but we cannot be sure based on just the graph. If we look at the differences, we see that the first differences are* $55.5, 27.5, -0.5, -28.5$. *Then, the second differences are consistently* $28$. *Yes, this is a quadratic relationship.*

*Since we know* $(0, 0)$ *is on the graph, the constant of the quadratic function is* $0$. *Now we can use a system of two linear equations to find the symbolic representation:*

$$M(t) = at^2 + bt + 0$$

*Substituting* $(0.5, 55.5) \rightarrow 55.5 = 0.25a + 0.5b$

$\rightarrow 222 = a + 2b$ *[Multiply both sides by 4 to eliminate the decimals.]*

*Substituting* $(1, 83) \rightarrow 83 = a + b$

$$a + 2b = 222$$
$$\underline{-a - b = -83}$$
$$b = 139$$

so $a + 139 = 83 \rightarrow a = -56$

$M(t) = -56t^2 + 139t$

*We set the function equal to zero and find the other zero of the function to be: $x = 0$ or $2.48$ hours. For this context $2.48$ hours makes sense. In hours and minutes, the patient must remain inactive for 2 hours and 29 minutes.*

*The function is a good model to use for answering this question since the graph requires some speculation and estimation.*

*Alternatively, students may generate a model by estimating the location of the vertex at about $(1.25, 84)$, and then using the vertex form of a quadratic equation. Using this method results in an equation of approximately $f(x) = -50(x - 1.25)2 + 84$. A useful extension activity could be to compare these two methods and models.*

b. What is the highest concentration of medicine in the patient's blood?

*Using the symmetry of the zeros of the function, we find the vertex to be at the midpoint between them, or at $(1.24, 86.25)$. So the highest concentration will be $86.25$ ml.*

3. A student is conducting an experiment and, as time passes, the number of cells in the experiment decreases. How many cells will there be after 16 minutes?

| Time (minutes) | Cells |
|:---:|:---:|
| 0 | 5,000,000 |
| 1 | 2,750,000 |
| 2 | 1,512,500 |
| 3 | 831,875 |
| 4 | 457,531 |
| 5 | 251,642 |
| 6 | 138,403 |

*If we divide each term by the one before it we see that this is a geometric sequence where the rate is $0.55$ and the initial value is $5,000,000$. Therefore, we can represent this sequence symbolically by*
$c(m) = 5,000,000(0.55)^{m-1}$

$c(16) = 5,000,000(0.55)^{16-1} \rightarrow c(16) = 5,000,000(0.55)^{16-1} \rightarrow c(16) = 637.40 \ cells$

## Closing (1 minute)

**Lesson Summary**

When given a data set, strategies that could be used to determine the type of function that describes the relationship between the data are:

- Determine the variables involved and plot the points.

- After making sure the $x$-values are given at regular intervals, look for common differences between the data points – first and second.

- Determine the type of sequence the data models first, then use the general form of the function equation to find the parameters for the symbolic representation of the function.

## Exit Ticket (4 minutes)

Name _____    Date_____

# Lesson 6:  Modeling a Context From Data

Exit Ticket

1.  Lewis' dad put 1,000 dollars in a money market fund with a fixed interest rate when he was 16.  Lewis can't touch the money until he is 26, but he gets updates on the balance of his account.

| Years After Lewis Turns 16 | Account Balance in Dollars |
|---|---|
| 0 | 1000 |
| 1 | 1100 |
| 2 | 1210 |
| 3 | 1331 |
| 4 | 1464 |

   a.   Develop a model for this situation.

   b.   Use your model to determine how much Lewis will have when he turns 26 years old.

   c.   Comment on the limitations/validity of your model.

Exit Ticket Sample Solutions

1.  Lewis' dad put $1,000$ dollars in a money market fund when he was 16. Lewis can't touch the money until he is 26, but he gets updates on the balance of his account.

    | Years After Lewis Turns 16 | Account Balance in Dollars |
    |:---:|:---:|
    | 0 | 1000 |
    | 1 | 1100 |
    | 2 | 1210 |
    | 3 | 1331 |
    | 4 | 1464 |

    a.  Develop a model for this situation.

        *We might try graphing this data. However, in the viewing window that shows our data points (see graph below), it appears that the function might be linear. Let's try zooming out to see more of the key features of this graph (See graph below.)*

        $x$: $[0, 5]$     $y$: $[975, 1500]$

        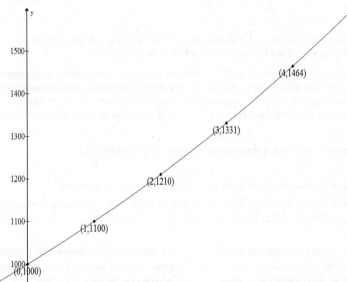

        *This viewing window gives us a close-up of the data points and their relation to each other. However, we cannot really see the features of the graph that represents the data.*

$x: [-25, 25] \quad y: [0, 9700]$

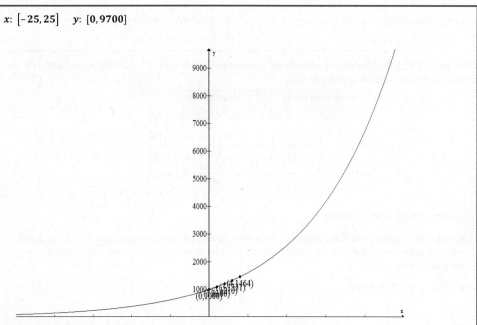

*In this version of the graph, you can see how the data from our table is grouped on a very short section of the graph. From this view, we can see the exponential nature of the graph.*

*Using the data table to find a function model: The first and second differences have no commonalities; therefore, this is not linear or quadratic. Checking to see if there is a common ratio, we see that this is an exponential relationship (or a geometric sequence) where the common ratio is 1.1, and the initial value is 1000. Check: Since on this table time starts at $t = 0$, using t as the exponent will yield $1000 for the initial balance.*

*Therefore, we can represent this sequence symbolically by:* $A(t) = 1000(1.1)^t$

b. Use your model to determine how much Lewis will have when he turns 26 years old.

*Using the function: Since Lewis will be 26 ten years after he turns 16, we will need to evaluate $A(10)$:*
$$A(10) = 1000(1.1)^{10} \rightarrow A(10) = 1000(1.1)^{10} \rightarrow A(10) = 2593.74 \text{ or } \$2,593.74$$

*We might also try extending our data table to verify this result. There are a couple of precision decisions to make: Shall we use 1.1 as the common ratio? How soon should we begin rounding numbers off? For this table, we decided to use 1.1 as the common ratio and did not round until the final step.*

*We might also try to answer this question using our graph. Below is another view of the graph. Can you estimate the balance at $t = 10$?*

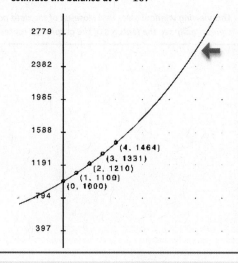

| Lewis' Age | Years After Lewis Turns 16 | Account Balance in Dollars |
|---|---|---|
| 16 | 0 | 1000 |
| 17 | 1 | 1100 |
| 18 | 2 | 1210 |
| 19 | 3 | 1331 |
| 20 | 4 | 1464.1 |
| 21 | 5 | 1610.51 |
| 22 | 6 | 1771.56 |
| 23 | 7 | 1948.72 |
| 24 | 8 | 2143.59 |
| 25 | 9 | 2357.95 |
| 26 | 10 | 2593.74 |

c.  Comment on the limitations/validity of your model.

*As we saw in the first and second versions of the graph, there are limitations to the graphic model because we cannot always see the key features of the graph in a window that lets us see all the data points clearly. Being able to see the graph using both windows was more helpful. Then, in part (b), we saw how difficult it was to estimate the value of the function at $t = 10$ for such large numbers of $A(t)$. We were also able to extend the table without too much difficulty, after deciding what level of precision we needed to use.*

*The equation was most helpful, but requires interpretation of both the data (noticing that the common ratio was very close but not absolutely perfect, and making sure we started with $t = 0$), and the results (rounding to indicate money).*

# Lesson 7:  Modeling a Context from Data

## Student Outcomes

- Students use linear, quadratic, and exponential functions to model data from tables, and choose the regression most appropriate to a given context.  They use the correlation coefficient to determine the accuracy of a regression model and then interpret the function in context. They then make predictions based on their model, and use an appropriate level of precision for reporting results and solutions.

## Lesson Notes

Lesson 7 focuses on data sets that cannot be modeled accurately, and students are asked to articulate why.  Students use skills learned in Lesson 14 of Module 2 (where they used calculators to write linear regressions), and apply similar techniques for data sets that are better suited to modeling with quadratic or exponential regressions.  Students will use that same technique to find linear regressions, and use their graphing calculators to examine the correlation coefficient, and to find quadratic and exponential regressions. They will compare correlation coefficients to determine which model is best for the data. Ultimately, students choose the regression model (linear, quadratic, or exponential) most appropriate to a given data set and then write, verify, and interpret these models in context.  Students will need a graphing calculator to complete this lesson.

Refer to the following full modeling cycle during this lesson. (Found on page 61 of the CCLS and page 72 of the CCSS):

> **Scaffolding:**
> - Students will be more engaged when working with relevant and real data that interests them. Websites that provide data sets are a good resource for classroom investigations.
> - This lesson might need to be divided into two days if students need more time to master the technology.

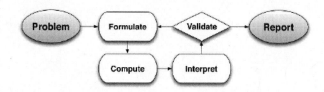

Classwork

## Opening Exercise (5 minutes)

Display the following data set, which cannot be modeled precisely. Ask the first question to start a class discussion.

---

**Opening Exercise**

**What is this data table telling us?**

| Age (Years) | NYC Marathon Running Time (Minutes) |
|:-----------:|:-----------------------------------:|
| 15 | 300 |
| 25 | 190 |
| 35 | 180 |
| 45 | 200 |
| 55 | 225 |
| 65 | 280 |

*The relationship between the age of runners in the NYC Marathon and their running time.*

---

(Note: In answering the question above, students may give more detail about the structure of the data and the relationships between the numbers. Let them brainstorm, but guide them to use the title of the table to inform them and not to read between the lines too much.)

After an initial discussion of the table, read the questions aloud and have students independently write their answers to the following questions:

- What function type appears to be best suited to modeling this data? Why do you think so?
    - *It looks like this data might be modeled by a quadratic function or absolute value function because it decreases, reaches a minimum, and then increases again.*

- Can we model this data precisely using the methods learned in previous lessons? Why or why not?
    - *These specific data points cannot be modeled precisely by a linear function or absolute value function because even though the x-values are given at regular intervals, there is not a common first difference (on either side of the 'vertex') in the function values. Nor can the data be modeled by a quadratic function, because the second differences are not exactly the same. An exponential function will not work either, because there is not a common ratio between consecutive terms.*

- What questions might we want to ask, using the given data and its model(s)?
    - *Let students brainstorm the possibilities. Here are a few possibilities: How was the data collected? How many total data points are there? Are these running times averages? What is a realistic domain? Is it reasonable to include ages less than 15? How about ages greater than 56? [Note: Later in this lesson, we will look at the data and ask what the peak age is for running the marathon.]*

(Note: At this point, to highlight MP.1 and MP.4, consider providing graph paper and asking students to informally generate their own functions to model the data. These can then be compared with those found by the calculator.)

## Example 1 (15 minutes)

Remind students that most real-world data is messy and imperfect, like the examples they worked with in Module 2. Frequently, statisticians use technology to find the function model (linear, quadratic, etc.) that *best* fits the data, even if the fit is not perfect.  In this lesson, students analyze regressions by considering the correlation coefficient, and use regression models to answer questions and make predictions about the data.  Remind students of the procedure they used in Lesson 14 of Module 2 to write linear regressions.

---

**Example 1**

Remember that in Module 2, we used a graphing display calculator (GDC) to find a linear regression model.  If a linear model is not appropriate for a collection of data, it may be possible that a quadratic or exponential will be a better fit.  Your graphing calculator is capable of determining various types of regressions.  Use a graphing display calculator (GDC) to determine if a data set has a better fit with a quadratic or exponential function.  You may need to review entering the data into the stats application of your GDC.

When you are ready to begin, return to the data presented in the Opening Exercise.  Use your graphing calculator to determine the function that best fits the data.  Then, answer some questions your teacher will ask about the data.

---

*Scaffolding:*

Some students may need to review this calculator procedure from Module 2 before extending it to include quadratic or exponential regressions. If your students use a different type of calculator, you will need to modify these instructions:

**Finding the Regression Line (TI-84 Plus)**
     **Step 1:**  From your home screen, press **STAT.**
     **Step 2:**  From the **STAT** menu, select the **EDIT** option. (**EDIT** enter)
     **Step 3:**  Enter the x-values of the data set in L1.
     **Step 4:**  Enter the y-values of the data set in L2.
     **Step 5:**  Select **STAT**.  Move cursor to the menu item **CALC,** and then move the cursor to option 4: LinReg($ax + b$) or option 8: LinReg($a + bx$).  Press enter.  (Discuss with students that both options 4 and 8 are representations of a linear equation.  Most students should be familiar with option 4, or the slope $y$-intercept form.  Option 8 is essentially the same representation using a different letter to represent slope and $y$-intercept. Option 8 is the preferred option in statistical studies.)
     **Step 6:**  With option 4 or option 8 on the screen, enter L1, L2, and Y1 as described in the following notes. LinReg($a + bx$) L1, L2, Y1

Select enter to see results.  The least-squares regression will be stored in Y1.  Work with students in graphing the scatter plot and Y1.

**Note:** L1 represents the $x$-values of the regression function, L2 the $y$-values, and Y1 represents the function of the least squares regression function.

To obtain Y1, go to **VARS**, move cursor to **Y-VARS**, and then Functions (enter).  You are now at the screen highlighting the Y-variables.  Move cursor to Y1 and hit enter.
Y1 is the linear regression line, and will be stored in Y1.

---

First, it is important to explain that the quantity $r$, called the correlation coefficient, measures the strength and the direction of a linear relationship between two variables. If the data appears to be quadratic or exponential, then your calculator may also show you the coefficient of determination, $r^2$. We can use the correlation coefficient for nonlinear relationships to determine which is the best fit, but we should never rely solely on the statistical correlation for nonlinear data. It is always important to also look at the scatter plot of the data along with the graph of the regression equation.

Finding a Regression Equation (TI-83 Plus)

Start with the same steps that you used for a linear regression.

**Step 1**: From your home screen, press STAT.

**Step 2**: From the STAT menu, select the EDIT option. (EDIT enter)

**Step 3**: Enter the $x$-values of the data set in L1.

**Step 4**: Enter the $y$-values of the data set in L2.

| Hours since observation began | Number of bacteria present |
|---|---|
| 0 | 20 |
| 1 | 40 |
| 2 | 75 |
| 3 | 150 |
| 4 | 297 |
| 5 | 510 |

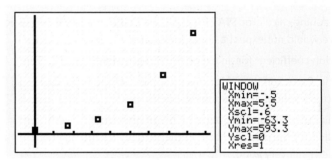

[The example below shows the number of bacteria cells growing in a laboratory.]

*After Step 4, however, the procedure changes. Instead of choosing option 4: LinReg(ax + b), students will choose option 5: QuadReg, or option 0: ExpReg, depending on which type of function appears to be most likely.*

**Step 5**: Press [STAT]. Select menu item CALC and then select option 5: ExpReg. Press [ENTER].

**Step 6**: With ExpReg on the home screen, press [VARS] and select Y-VARS, FUNCTION, Y1 and press [ENTER] so that ExpReg Y1 is displayed on the home screen. Select [ENTER] to see results. The quadratic regression will be stored in Y1.

**Step 7**: To graph both the regression and the scatter plot of data, fit the window to match the parameters of the data set, and also to make sure that PLOT1 and Y1 are highlighted on the [Y=] screen.

*Note to teachers:*

To find the coefficient of determination $r^2$, search the CATALOG by pressing [2$^{ND}$][0], selecting DIAGNOSTIC ON, and pressing [ENTER][ENTER]. Once the diagnostic is turned on, every time students find a regression, the coefficient of determination $r^2$ will be listed at the bottom of the screen.

In the example below, we can see that the exponential function that closely models this data is approximately:

$f(x) = (20.51)(1.92)^x$, and that the correlation coefficient is 0.9989...

Also remember that once the function is graphed in your calculator, you can use the TRACE function to find specific values.

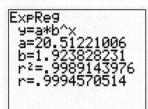

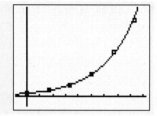

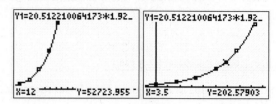

Now we return to the data we looked at in the Opening Exercise.

- Point out: We learned in Module 2 that a correlation coefficient close to 1 or $-1$ indicates that a regression line fits the data closely; the closer that $r^2$ is to 0, the less effective the regression will be at modeling the data and making predictions about the future. Have students use their graphing calculators to analyze the data from the Opening Exercise.

- Using the graphing calculator STAT function, we find that a linear regression has a correlation coefficient of $-0.32$, so we would not expect a linear function to model this data well.

- The correlation coefficient for an exponential regression is $-0.37$. This is also not expected to be a good fit.

- The quadratic regression model for this example is $f(x) = 0.172x^2 - 13.714x + 451.763$, which has a correlation coefficient of approximately $-0.94$.

Here is the graph of the data and the regression equation from two different views. In the first, we can see that the function is a good fit for the data we have. In the second, we zoom in on a few points and realize that, although the fit is not perfect, it is still very good.

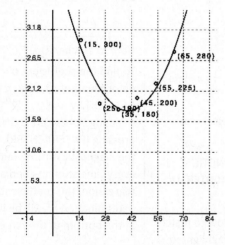

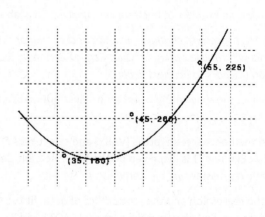

- With how much accuracy do we need to approximate our results for this modeling function? For instance, if our leading coefficient is 0.1723214286, does that mean we have to round our answers in minutes to the ten-billionth decimal place?

    ▫ *Typically, we can round to the same place value that our data was given in. Because our data set is originally given in terms of whole minutes, it is perfectly reasonable to round our answers to whole minutes as well.*

MP.6

**Important Note:** Keep in mind that rounding your answers to the nearest whole number does not mean you can round your coefficients to the same place value; in this example, that would mean rounding our *a* coefficient from 0.17… to 0, eliminating the quadratic term. For the regression coefficients, round to at least the hundredths or thousandths place, and further if the number is even smaller, or risk diminishing the accuracy of the model.

- Our model lies entirely in the first quadrant, and the model function has no (real) roots. Why is this?

  - *It would be impossible to run the marathon in 0 minutes or less, and it is impossible for age to be represented by a negative number.*

- According to this data, what is the peak age for running the marathon? In other words, what is the approximate best age for the shortest run time of this modeling function? What does this represent in the context of this problem? Do you find this data to be unusual in any way? If so, how?

  - *The vertex of our modeling function is approximately* $(40, 179)$*, meaning that the lowest possible marathon time of* $179$ *minutes would be expected to be run by a* $40$*-year-old, according to the model. This data could be interpreted as being somewhat strange because one might argue that the average* $40$*-year-old is not as physically fit as the average* $25$*- or* $30$*-year-old.*

- Based on this regression model, how long might it take the average 50-year-old to run the NYC marathon?

  - *By substituting* $x = 50$ *into our regression model, we get* $f(50) = 196$ *minutes.*

## Exercise 1–2 (20 minutes)

Have students work with a partner or small group to answer the questions about the data set provided below. Then use the questions that follow to guide a class discussion in which you might call on students to share their answers.

---

Exercises

1. Use the following data table to construct a regression model, then answer the questions:

| Chicken Breast Frying Time (Minutes) | Moisture Content (%) |
|---|---|
| 5 | 16.3 |
| 10 | 9.7 |
| 15 | 8.1 |
| 20 | 4.2 |
| 25 | 3.4 |
| 30 | 2.9 |
| 45 | 1.9 |
| 60 | 1.3 |

Data Source: *Journal of Food Processing and Preservation*, 1995.

a. What function type appears to be the best fit for this data? Explain how you know.

*The relationship between frying time and moisture content is best modeled by an exponential regression. Using the calculator yields the function* $f(x) = 13.895 - 0.957^x$ *with a coefficient of determination of approximately* $0.904$. *[$r = -0.95077…$ so $R^2 = 0.9039…$].*

b. A student chooses a quadratic regression to model this data. Is he right or wrong? Why or why not?

*This data cannot be modeled by quadratic regression because as cooking time increases, moisture content will always decrease and never begin to increase again. Also, in looking at the longer-term trend, we see that for a quadratic model the values are decreasing initially but will eventually begin to increase. This makes the quadratic model less reliable for larger x-values.*

---

Lesson 7:    Modeling a Context from Data
Date:      10/4/13

c.    Will the moisture content for this product ever reach 0%?  Why or why not?

*The moisture content will never reach 0%, because exponential decay functions get smaller and smaller, but never disappear entirely.  Also, it doesn't make sense for something to have absolutely NO moisture in it.*

d.    Based on this model, what would you expect the moisture content to be of a chicken breast fried for 50 minutes?

$f(50) = 13.895(0.957^{50}) = 1.5\%$ *moisture content for a chicken breast fried for 50 min.*

2.    Use the following data table to construct a regression model, then answer the questions based on your model.

Prevalence of No Leisure-Time Activities, 1988 - 2008

| Year | Years since 1988 | % of prevalence |
|------|------------------|-----------------|
| 1988 | 0 | 30.5 |
| 1989 | 1 | 31.5 |
| 1990 | 2 | 30.9 |
| 1991 | 3 | 30.6 |
| 1992 | 4 | 29.3 |
| 1994 | 6 | 30.2 |
| 1996 | 8 | 28.4 |
| 1998 | 10 | 28.4 |
| 2000 | 12 | 27.8 |
| 2001 | 13 | 26.2 |
| 2002 | 14 | 25.1 |
| 2003 | 15 | 24.2 |
| 2004 | 16 | 23.7 |
| 2005 | 17 | 25.1 |
| 2006 | 18 | 23.9 |
| 2007 | 19 | 23.9 |
| 2008 | 20 | 25.1 |

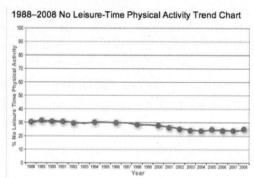

1988–2008 No Leisure-Time Physical Activity Trend Chart

*Using technology to find a linear regression model, we find that the best-fit line is $y = -0.3988x + 31.517$, with a correlation coefficient of $-0.952$.*

a.    What trends do you see in this collection of data?

*The data seem to be dropping gradually over the years, but at a fairly constant, though small, negative rate. The correlation coefficient of nearly $-1$ indicates that this model has a strong negative linear relationship.*

b.    How do you interpret this trend?

*The rate of leisure-time physical activity in the U.S. has slowly declined over the years since 1988, and is likely to continue to do so.*

c.    If the trend continues, what would we expect the percentage of people in the U.S. who report no leisure-time physical activity to be in 2020?

*The year 2020 is year 32, since 1988, so $f(32) = -0.3988(32) + 31.517 = 18.755$. So, if this trend continues, we would expect about 19% of the population to report no leisure-time physical activity in 2020.*

## Closing (2 minutes)

- Data plots and other visual displays of data can help us determine the function type that appears to be the best fit for the data.

- When faced with messy real world data sets, it is relatively easy to use technology to find the best possible fit for a function to model the data.

- We can also experiment with transforming a parent function to manually create a model.

---

**Lesson Summary**

- Using data plots and other visual displays of data the function type that appears to be the best fit for the data can be determined. Using the correlation coefficient the measure of the strength and the direction of a linear relationship can be determined.

- A graphing calculator can be used if the data sets are imperfect. To find a regression equation, the same steps will be performed as for a linear regression.

---

## Exit Ticket (5 minutes)

Name _____     Date_____

# Lesson 7:  Modeling a Context From Data

Exit Ticket

1.  Use the following data table to construct a regression model, then answer the questions:

| Shoe Length (inches) | Height (inches) |
|---|---|
| 11.4 | 68 |
| 11.6 | 67 |
| 11.8 | 65 |
| 11.8 | 71 |
| 12.2 | 69 |
| 12.2 | 69 |
| 12.2 | 71 |
| 12.6 | 72 |
| 12.6 | 74 |
| 12.8 | 70 |

a.   What is the best regression model for the data?

b.   Based on your regression model, what height would you expect a person with a shoe length of 13.4 inches to be?

c.   Interpret the value of your correlation coefficient in the context of the problem.

## Exit Ticket Sample Solutions

1.  Use the following data table to construct a regression model then answer the questions:

| Shoe Length (inches) | Height (inches) |
|---|---|
| 11.4 | 68 |
| 11.6 | 67 |
| 11.8 | 65 |
| 11.8 | 71 |
| 12.2 | 69 |
| 12.2 | 69 |
| 12.2 | 71 |
| 12.6 | 72 |
| 12.6 | 74 |
| 12.8 | 70 |

a.  What is the best regression model for the data?

*The best model for regression here is linear, modeled using the calculator as $f(x) = 3.657x + 25.277$ with a correlation coefficient of $0.6547$.*

b.  Based on your regression model, what height would you expect a person with a shoe length of $13.4$ inches to be?

*$f(13.4) = 74 \rightarrow$ a person with shoes $13.4$ inches long might be $74$ inches tall.*

c.  Interpret the value of your correlation coefficient in the context of the problem.

*Based on the correlation coefficient, there is a moderate positive linear relationship between shoe length and height.*

## Problem Set Sample Solutions

1.  Use the following data tables to write a regression model, then answer the questions:

**Prescription Drug Sales in the United States Since 1995**

| Years Since 1995 | Prescription Drug Sales (billions of $USD) |
|---|---|
| 0 | 68.6 |
| 2 | 81.9 |
| 3 | 103.0 |
| 4 | 121.7 |
| 5 | 140.7 |

a.  What is the best model for this data?

*The best model for this data would be an exponential regression, given by the function $f(t) = 65.736(1.161)^t$ with a correlation coefficient of $0.987$.*

b.  Based on your model, what would you expect prescription drug sales to be in 2002? 2005?

*2002: $f(7) = 186.9$, and 2005: $f(10) = 292.5$*

| Lesson 7: | Modeling a Context from Data |
|---|---|
| Date: | 10/4/13 |

c. For this model, would it make sense to input negative values for *t* into your regression? Why or why not?

*Because there were prescription drug sales in the years prior to 1995, it would make sense to use negative numbers with this model. (Unless some drastic change in drug sales in 1995 makes this model inaccurate for preceding years.)*

2. Use the data below to answer the questions that follow:

Per Capita Ready-to-Eat Cereal Consumption in the United States per Year Since 1980

| Years Since 1980 | Cereal Consumption (lb.) | Years Since 1980 | Cereal Consumption (lb.) |
|---|---|---|---|
| 0 | 12 | 10 | 15.4 |
| 1 | 12 | 11 | 16.1 |
| 2 | 11.9 | 12 | 16.6 |
| 3 | 12.2 | 13 | 17.3 |
| 4 | 12.5 | 14 | 17.4 |
| 5 | 12.8 | 15 | 17.1 |
| 6 | 13.1 | 16 | 16.6 |
| 7 | 13.3 | 17 | 16.3 |
| 8 | 14.2 | 18 | 15.6 |
| 9 | 14.9 | 19 | 15.5 |

a. What is the best model for this data?

*The best regression fit here is the quadratic $f(t) = -0.018t^2 + 0.637t + 10.797$ with correlation coefficient of $0.92$ and a coefficient of determination ($R^2$) of $0.85$.*

b. Based on your model, what would you expect per capita cereal consumption to be in 2002? 2005?

*According to the model, $f(22) = 16.1$ lb. of cereal, and $f(25) = 15.5$ lb.*

*(Note: Because this model has a little lower coefficient of determination ($0.85$), these predictions may not seem to fit well with the given data table.)*

c. For this model, will it make sense to input *t*-values that return negative $f(t)$-values into your regression? Why or why not?

*No, $f(t)$ values for this model would correspond to negative pounds of cereal consumed, which is impossible. Therefore, this model would only be useful over the domain where $f(t)$ is positive.*

Lesson 7:    Modeling a Context from Data
Date:      10/4/13

102

# Lesson 8:  Modeling a Context from a Verbal Description

## Student Outcomes

- Students model functions described verbally in a given context using graphs, tables, or algebraic representations.

## Lesson Notes

In this lesson, students use the full modeling cycle to model functions described verbally in the context of business and commerce.  Throughout this lesson, refer to the modeling cycle depicted below.  (As seen on page 61 of the CCLS and page 72 of the CCSS.)

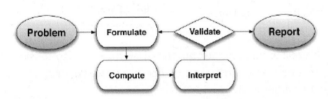

**Standards for Mathematical Practice:**  Throughout this lesson students are asked to use the full modeling cycle in looking for entry points to the solution, formulating a model, performing accurate calculations, interpreting the model and the function, and validating and reporting their results.

> *Scaffolding:*
>
> Remind students of the formulas they used in Lesson 3 of this module and in Module 4 related to business, compound interest, and population growth and decay.  If students need a review, you may want to take them back to that lesson for an Opening Exercise.

## Classwork

Use these two examples to remind students of the formulas used in applications related to business.

### Example 1 (8 minutes)

Have students to work in pairs or small groups to solve the following problem.  You may want to use this as a guided exercise depending on the needs of your students.

---

**Example 1**

Christine has $500 to deposit in a savings account and she is trying to decide between two banks.  Bank A offers 10% annual interest compounded quarterly.  Rather than compounding interest for smaller accounts, Bank B offers to add $15 quarterly to any account with a balance of less than $1000 for every quarter, as long as there are no withdrawals.  Christine has decided that she will neither withdraw, nor make a deposit for a number of years.

Develop a model that will help Christine decide which bank to use.

---

Students may decide to use a table, graph, or equation to model this situation. For this situation, a table allows us to compare the balances at the two banks. Here we see that Bank B has a higher balance until the fourth year.

| At Year End | Bank A Balance | Bank B Balance |
|---|---|---|
| Year 1 | $551.90 | $560 |
| Year 2 | $609.20 | $620 |
| Year 3 | $672.44 | $680 |
| Year 4 | $742.25 | $740 |

*Scaffolding:*

If students need some scaffolding for this example, you might try breaking down the entry to the problem into steps. For example, the first question might be:

**How will we use the fact that the interest is compounded quarterly when we create the model?**

*In the formula for compounded interest, we will use 4t for the exponent, since the interest will be compounded 4 times each year. And we will divide the annual interest rate of 10% by 4.*

Then, walk students through the solution steps.

We might be tempted to just say that at more than 3 years Bank A is better. If students reach this conclusion, use the following line of questioning:

- Can we give a more exact answer? Since the interest is compounded quarterly, we may want to consider the quarters of year 3. If after choosing a bank, Christine wanted to make sure her money was earning as much as possible, after which quarter would she make the withdrawal?

  - *Since the balances intersect in year 4, we can look at the balances for each quarter of that year:*

| Year 3 - Quarters | Bank A | Bank B |
|---|---|---|
| Year 3 | $672.44 | $680 |
| 1st | $689.26 | $695 |
| 2nd | $706.49 | $710 |
| 3rd | $724.15 | $725 |
| 4th | $742.25 | $740 |

  - *We can see from this table that it isn't until the 4th quarter that Bank A begins to make more money for Christine. If she chooses Bank A, she should leave her money there for more than 3 years. If she chooses Bank B, she should withdraw before the 4th quarter of Year 3.*

Note: If students prefer to use the function as a model for Example 1:

Bank A: $A(t) = 500 \left(1 + \frac{0.10}{4}\right)^{4t}$ or $500(1.025)^{4t}$

Bank B: $B(t) = 500 + 60t$ *(Since her money earns $15 quarterly, then $15(4) = $60 a year.)*

## Example 2 (8 minutes)

**Example 2**

Alex designed a new snowboard. He wants to market it and make a profit. The total initial cost for manufacturing set-up, advertising, etc. is $500,000$ and the materials to make the snowboards cost $100$ per board.

The demand function for selling a similar snowboard is: $D(p) = 50,000 - 100p$, where $p$ = selling price of each snowboard.

a.  Write an expression for each of the following. Let $p$ represent the selling price:

Demand Function (number of units that will sell)

*This is given as* $50,000 - 100p$.

Revenue (number of units that will sell, price per unit, $p$)

$(50,000 - 100p)p = 50,000p - 100p^2$

Total Cost (cost for producing the snowboards)

*This is the total overhead costs, plus the cost per snowboard times the number of snowboards:*

$500,000 + 100(50,000 - 100p)$

$500,000 + 5,000,000 - 10,000p$

$5,500,000 - 10,000p$

b.  Write an expression to represent the profit.

$Profit = Total\ Revenue - Total\ Cost\ [f(p)]$

$(50,000p - 100p^2) - (5,500,000 - 10,000p)$

*Therefore, the profit function is* $f(p) = -100p^2 + 60,000p - 5,500,000$.

c.  What is the selling price of the snowboard that will give the maximum profit?

*Solve for the vertex of the quadratic function using completing the square.*

$$f(p) = -100p^2 + 60,000p - 5,500,000$$
$$= -100(p^2 - 600p + \quad) - 5,500,000$$
$$= -100(p^2 - 600p + 300^2) - 5,500,000 + 100(300)^2$$
$$= -100(p - 300)^2 - 5,500,000 + 9,000,000$$
$$= -100(p - 300)^2 + 3,500,000$$

*So, the selling price that will yield the maximum profit is at* $p = \$300$.

d.  What is the maximum profit Alex can make?

*According to the vertex form, the maximum profit would be $3,500,000 for selling at a price of $300 for each snowboard.*

## Exercises 1–2 (20 minutes)

Have students work in pairs or small groups to solve the following two exercises. You may want to anticipate the needs of your students by heading off any issues you foresee arising in these problems. For example, in part (d) of the first exercise, students will need to model using a table of values or a graph since they are not experienced with solving exponential equations. You may need to remind them that sometimes a table is the preferred model for solving a problem since graphs often require rough estimates. They may need to set up a program in their calculator, or use a spreadsheet. Calculators and/or graph paper will be important for these exercises. Table building and other calculations will require a scientific calculator, at the very least. For example, in part (c) of Exercise 2, students will need to take a 5$^{th}$ root of 2.

---

**Exercises**

Alvin just turned 16 years old. His grandmother told him that she will give him $10,000$ to buy any car he wants whenever he is ready. Alvin wants to be able to buy his dream car by his 21$^{st}$ birthday and he wants a 2009 Avatar Z, which he could purchase today for $25,000$. The car depreciates (reduces in value) at a rate is $15\%$ per year. He wants to figure out how long it would take for his $10,000$ to be enough to buy the car, without investing it.

1.  Write the function that models the depreciated value of the car after $n$ number of years?

$$f(n) = \$25,000(1 - 0.15)^n \text{ or } f(n) = 25,000(0.85)^n$$

| After $n$ years | Value of the Car |
|:---:|:---:|
| 1 | $21,250$ |
| 2 | $18,062.5$ |
| 3 | $15,353.13$ |
| 4 | $13,050.16$ |
| 5 | $11,092.63$ |
| 6 | $9428.74$ |

a.  Will he be able to afford to buy the car when he turns 21? Explain why or why not.

$$f(n) = 25,000(0.85)^n$$

$$f(5) = 25,000(0.85)^5 = \$11,092.63 \dots$$

*No, he will not be able to afford to buy the car in 5 years because the value of the car will still be $11,092.63$, and he has only $10,000$.*

b.  Given the same rate of depreciation, after how many years will the value of the car be less than $5000$?

$$f(10) = 25,000(0.85)^{10} = \$4921.86$$

*In 10 years, the value of the car will be less than $5,000$.*

c.  If the same rate of depreciation were to continue indefinitely, after how many years would the value of the car be approximately $1$?

$$F(n) = 25,000(0.85)^n = 1$$

*In about 62 years the value of the car is approximately $1$.*

---

**Scaffolding:**

- Remind students that we used quarterly compounding in Example 1 of this lesson.

- Depending on the needs of your students, you may want to do a scaffolded introduction to this problem, helping them get the set up, and maybe even discuss the functions.

---

| Lesson 8: | Modeling a Context from a Verbal Description |
|---|---|
| Date: | 10/4/13 |

2. Sophia plans to invest $1000 in each of three banks.

Bank A offers an annual interest rate of 12%, compounded annually.

Bank B offers an annual interest rate of 12%, compounded quarterly.

Bank C offers an annual interest rate of 12%, compounded monthly.

a. Write the function that describes the growth of investment for each bank in $n$ years?

*Bank A* $\qquad A(n) = 1000(1.12)^n$

*Bank B* $\qquad B(n) = 1000\left(1 + \frac{0.12}{12}\right)^{4n}$ *or* $1000(1.03)^{4n}$

*Bank C* $\qquad C(n) = 1000\left(1 + \frac{0.12}{12}\right)^{12n}$ *or* $1000(1.01)^{12n}$

b. How many years will it take to double her initial investment for each bank? (Round to the nearest whole dollar.)

| Year | Bank A | Bank B | Bank C |
|------|--------|--------|--------|
| Year 1 | $1120 | $1126 | $1127 |
| Year 2 | $1254 | $1267 | $1270 |
| Year 3 | $1405 | $1426 | $1431 |
| Year 4 | $1574 | $1605 | $1612 |
| Year 5 | $1762 | $1806 | $1817 |
| Year 6 | $1974 | $2033 | $2047 |
| Year 7 | $2210.68 | $2288 | $2307 |

*For Bank A, her money will double after 7 years.*

*For Banks B and C, her investment will double its value during the 6th year.*

c. Sophia went to Bank D. The bank offers a "double your money program" for an initial investment of $1000 in five years, compounded annually. What is the annual interest rate for Bank D?

*Given information for Bank D:*

*Initial investment =* $1000

*Number of Years = 5 (She would have* $2000 *in 5 years.)*

*Compounded annually. So,*

$$2 \times 1000 = 1000(1 + r)^5$$
$$2000 = 1000(1 + r)^5$$
$$\frac{2000}{1000} = \frac{1000(1 + r)^5}{1000}$$
$$2 = (1 + r)^5$$

*[Since we see that 2 is the 5th power of a number, we must take the 5th root of 2.]*

$$\sqrt[5]{2} = (1 + r)$$

$$1.1487 = 1 + r$$

$$1.1487 - 1 = r$$

$$r = 0.1487 \text{ or } 14.87\% \text{ [annual interest rate for Bank D]}$$

| Lesson 8: | Modeling a Context from a Verbal Description |
|-----------|---------------------------------------------|
| Date: | 10/4/13 |

107

## Closing (1 minute)

- Sometimes a graph or table is the best model for problems that involve complicated function equations.

---

**Lesson Summary**

- We can use the full modeling cycle is used to solve real world problems in the context of business and commerce (e.g., compound interest, revenue, profit, and cost) and population growth and decay (e.g., population growth, depreciation value, and half-life) to demonstrate linear, exponential, and quadratic functions described verbally through using graphs, tables, or algebraic expressions to make appropriate interpretation and decision.

- Sometimes a graph or table is the best model for problems that involve complicated function equations.

---

## Exit Ticket (6 minutes)

Name _____     Date_____

# Lesson 8:  Modeling a Context From a Verbal Description

Exit Ticket

Answer the following question.  Look back at this (or other) lessons if you need help with the business formulas.

Jerry and Carlos each have $1000 and are trying to increase their savings.  Jerry will keep his money at home and add $50 per month from his part time job.  Carlos will put his money in a bank account that earns a 4% yearly interest rate, compounded monthly.  Who has a better plan for increasing his savings?

## Exit Ticket Sample Solutions

**Answer the following question. Look back at this (or other) lessons if you need help with the business formulas.**

Jerry and Carlos each have $1000 and are trying to increase their savings. Jerry will keep his money at home and add $50 per month from his part time job. Carlos will put his money in a bank account that earns a 4% yearly interest rate, compounded monthly. Who has a better plan for increasing his savings?

*Jerry's savings:*   $J(n) = 1000 + 50(n)$, *where* $n$ = *number of months*

*Carlos' savings:*   $C(n) = 1000 \left(1 + \frac{0.04}{12}\right)^{12n}$, *where* $n$ = *number of months*

| Number of months | Jerry's savings | Carlos' savings (rounded to 2 decimals places) |
|:---:|:---:|:---:|
| 0 | $1000 | $1000 |
| 1 | $1050 | $1040.74 |
| 2 | $1100 | $1083.14 |
| 3 | $1150 | $1127.27 |
| 4 | $1200 | $1173.20 |
| ... | ... | ... |
| $n$ | $1000 + 50(n)$ | $1000\left(1 + \frac{0.04}{12}\right)^{12n}$ |

*In the short term, Jerry's plan is better; in the long term, Carlos's plan is better.*

## Problem Set Sample Solutions

Students will need a calculator to perform the necessary calculations for this problem set.

1.  Maria invested $10,000 in the stock market. Unfortunately, the value of her investment has been dropping at an average rate of 3% each year.

    a.  Write the function that best models the situation.

    $f(n) = 10,000(1 - 0.03)^\wedge n \ or \ 10,000(0.97)^n$
    *where* $n$ = *number of years since the initial investment*

    b.  If the trend continues, how much will her investment be worth in 5 years?

    For $n = 5$

    $f(n) = 10,000(0.97)^n$

    $f(5) = 10,000(0.97)^5$

    $f(5) = 8587.34 \ or \ \$8,587.34$

c.  Given the situation, what should she do with her investment?

*[There are multiple answers and there is no wrong answer.]  Sample Responses:*

*Answer 1:  After two years, I will pull out my money and invest it in another company.*

*Answer 2:  According to experts, I should not touch my investment and wait for it to bounce back.*

2.  The half-life of the radioactive material in Z-Med, a medication used for certain types of therapy, is 2 days.  A patient receives a 16-mCi dose (millicuries, a measure of radiation) in his treatment.  [Half-life means that the radioactive material decays to the point where only half is left.]

a.  Make a table to show the level of Z-Med in the patient's body after $n$ days.

| Number of days | Level of *Z-Med* in patient |
|:---:|:---:|
| 0 | 16 *mCi* |
| 2 | 8 *mCi* |
| 4 | 4 *mCi* |
| 6 | 2 *mCi* |
| 8 | 1 *mCi* |
| 10 | 0.5 *mCi* |

b.  Write an equation for $f(n)$ to model the half-life of *Z-Med* for $n$ days. [Be careful here.  Make sure that the formula works for both odd and even numbers of days.]

$$f(n) = 16 \left(\frac{1}{2}\right)^{\frac{n}{2}}$$

*where $n$ = number of days after the initial measurement of 16 mCi*

c.  How much radioactive material from *Z-Med* is left in the patient's body after 20 days of receiving the medicine?

*For $n = 20$*

$$f(20) = 16(0.5)^{10}$$

$$f(20) = 0.015625$$

*After ten days, there is $0.015625$ mCi of the radioactive material in Z-Med left in the patient's body.*

3.  Suppose a male and a female of a certain species of animal were taken to a deserted island.  The population of this species quadruples (multiplies by 4) every year.  Assume that the animals have an abundant food supply and no predators on the island.

a.  What is an equation that can be used to model the number of offspring the animals will produce?

$$f(x) = 2(4)^n$$

*where $n$ = number of years after their arrival at the island.*

**COMMON CORE**™

Lesson 8:
Date:

Modeling a Context from a Verbal Description
10/4/13

111

b. What will the population of the species be after 5 years?

| After $n$ years | Population |
|---|---|
| 0 | 2 |
| 1 | 8 |
| 2 | 32 |
| 3 | 128 |
| 4 | 512 |
| 5 | 2048 |

*In 5 years, the population of the animals will reach 2,048.*

c. Write an equation to find how many years it will take for the population of the animals to exceed 1 million. Find the number of years, either by using the equation or a table.

*Using the equation:* $2(4)^n = 1,000,000$

$4^n = 500,000$

*[Note: Students will likely be unable to solve this equation without using trial and error (educated guessing). They may come up with $2(4)^{9.5} = 1,048,576$ using this method.]*

| After $n$ years | Population |
|---|---|
| 0 | 2 |
| 1 | 8 |
| 2 | 32 |
| 3 | 128 |
| 4 | 512 |
| 5 | 2,048 |
| 6 | 8,192 |
| 7 | 32,768 |
| 8 | 131,072 |
| 9 | 524,288 |
| 10 | 2,097,152 |

4. The revenue of a company for a given month is represented as $R(x) = 1,500x - x^2$, and its costs as $C(x) = 1,500 + 1,000x$. What is the selling price, $x$, of their product that would yield the maximum profit? Show or explain your answer.

$P(x) = Revenue - Cost$

$P(x) = R(x) - C(x)$

$P(x) = (1500x - x^2) - (1500 + 1000x)$

$P(x) = -x^2 + 500x - 1500$

*Profit Function*

*To find the vertex, we can complete the square for the function:*

$P(x) = -x^2 + 500x - 1500$

$\quad = -1(x^2 - 500x + \quad) - 1500$      *Group the x-terms and factor out the $-1$.*

$\quad = -1(x^2 - 500x + 62,500) - 1500 + 62,500$      *Complete the square.*

$P(x) = -1(x - 250)^2 + 61,000$

*So, the maximum point will be $(250, 61,000)$, and the selling price should be $250 per unit to yield a maximum profit of $61,000.*

# Lesson 9: Modeling a Context from a Verbal Description

## Student Outcomes

- Students interpret the function and its graph and use them to answer questions related to the model, including calculating the rate of change over an interval, and always using an appropriate level of precision when reporting results.
- Students use graphs to interpret the function represented by the equation in terms of the context, and answer questions about the model using the appropriate level of precision in reporting results.

**Standards for Mathematical Practice:** This lesson addresses attending to precision when modeling in mathematics. The lesson begins with an explanation of what precision is and students practice attending to precision with math model practice sets.

## Lesson Notes

In this lesson, students use the full modeling cycle to model functions described verbally in a context. Since this is the final lesson of the year, you might want to use the examples and exercises of this lesson for independent work by your students. You might have groups work on the same problem, assign different problems for each group, or offer them a choice. Then, you might have them display their results and/or make a short presentation for the class. Discussion of the work could focus on the most efficient and/or elegant solution paths, and the level of precision used in the work and in the reporting. A class discussion around the Opening Exercise should precede the student work in this lesson, and the Precision questions in the examples should be used to guide further discussion of this topic.

Throughout this lesson, refer to the modeling cycle depicted below (as seen on page 61 of the CCLS and page 72 of the CCSS).

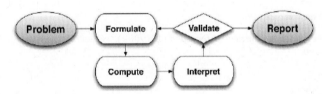

Classwork

> **Opening Exercise**
>
> What does it mean to "attend to precision" when modeling in mathematics?

## Examples 1 and 2 (10 minutes)

Have students read and plan a strategy for solving the problem below, before guiding the class through the problem. It is important to stress the three representations of a function (i.e., tabular, algebraic/symbolic, graphic), in addition to verbal description, and that certain contexts may require one, two, or all three.

> **Example 1**
>
> Marymount Township secured the construction of a power plant in 1990. Once the power plant was built, the population of Marymount increased by about 20% each year for the first ten years, and then increased by 5% each year after that.
>
> a.   If the population was 150,000 people in 2010, what was the population in 2000?
>
> *Sample Response: We can tell that this problem involves a geometric sequence because we are multiplying each term by either 1.2 or 1.05.*
>
> *This is also a piecewise function since the first ten years the population grows at one rate, and after that it grows at a different rate.*
>
> *We need to start backwards from 2010 to 2000, since we know the size of the population for 2010.*
>
> $$\text{Geometric sequence: } a_n = a_1 r^{n-1}$$
>
> *2000 to 2010*
>
> $$150,000 = a_1(1.05)^{11-1} \rightarrow 150,000 = a_1(1.05)^{10} \rightarrow 150,000/(1.05)^{10} = a_1 \rightarrow a_1 = 92086.99$$
> $$\approx 92,087$$
>
> **Precision**
>
> b.   How should you round your answer? Explain.
>
> *The 2010 value appears to be rounded to the nearest thousand (150,000). We will use a similar level of precision in our result: 92,000.*
>
> c.   What was the population in 1990?
>
> *Sample Response: For 1990 to 2000 we know the final population from our answer to part (a), so we can use that to find the initial population in 1990. [Note: For this sample response, we rounded off to 92,000 people.]*
>
> $$92087 = a_1(1.2)^{10} \rightarrow \frac{92087}{(1.2)^{10}} = a_1 \rightarrow a_1 = 14872.56, \text{ so } 15,000.$$

If you used the symbolic representation of the piecewise defined function, with $a_1 = 14{,}873$, the population estimate is 150,003.

- Is it okay that we came out with 3 more people in our model than we should have?

  □ *When the total is a number as large as* 150,000, *being off by* 3 *is permissible. In fact, if a population were exactly* 150,003, *most people would likely refer to the population as* 150,000.

- Point out: This is a great opportunity to explain to students why a slight change in geometric sequences can change the answer (sometimes dramatically, if the domain is large enough).

---

**Example 2**

**If the trend continued, what would the population be in 2009?**

*Sample response: Since that is one year before the end of our sample, we can divide* 150,000 *by* 1.05 *to find the value before it:*

$$\frac{150,000}{1.05} \approx 142,000$$

---

## Exercise 1–2  (10 minutes)

Have students work in pairs or small groups to solve these problems. If students need more support, you might use these as a guided exercise.

---

**Exercises**

1. A tortoise and a hare are having a race. The tortoise moves at 4 miles per hour. The hare travels at 10 miles per hour. Halfway through the race, the hare decides to take a 5-hour nap and then gets up and continues at 10 miles per hour.

   a. If the race is 40 miles long, who won the race? Support your answer with mathematical evidence.

   *The time for the tortoise to finish* $= \frac{40}{4} = 10$ *hours. The time for the hare to finish* $= \frac{40}{10} + 5 = 9$ *hours. So, the hare beat the tortoise by one hour.*

   b. How long (in miles) would the race have to be for there to be a tie between the two creatures, if the same situation (as described in Exercise 1) happened?

   *Sample solution: Let the tortoise's time be* $T_t$ *and hare's time be* $T_h$.

   $$T_t = \frac{D}{4}$$

   $$T_h = \frac{D}{10} + 5 \text{ (racing + napping)}$$

   *Since both creatures "finished the same distance D in the same TOTAL time"*

   $$T_t = T_h$$

   $$\frac{D}{4} = \frac{D}{10} + 5$$

   *Solve for D,*

   $$D = 33\frac{1}{3} \text{ miles.}$$

   *[Check:* $T_t = 8\frac{1}{3}$ *hours* $= T_h$]

---

Lesson 9: Modeling a Context from a Verbal Description
Date: 10/4/13

115

**2.** The graph on the right represents the value $V$ of a popular stock. Its initial value was \$12/share on day 0.

Note: The calculator uses $X$ to represent $t$, and $Y$ to represent $V$.

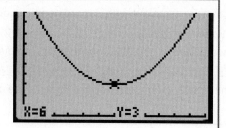

a. How many days after its initial value at time $t = 0$ did the stock price return to \$12 per share?

*By the symmetry of quadratic equations, the stock must return to its initial value after 6 more days, at $t = 12$.*

b. Write a quadratic equation representing the value of this stock over time.

*Since the quadratic equation reaches a minimum at $(6, 3)$ use vertex form to write $V = a(t - 6)^2 + 3$. The initial value at $t = 0$ was 12. So, by substitution $12 = a(0 - 6)^2 + 3 \rightarrow a = \frac{1}{4}$. Therefore, the final equation is $V = \frac{1}{4}(t - 6)^2 + 3$.*

c. Use this quadratic equation to predict the stock's value after 15 days.

$$V = \frac{1}{4}(15 - 6)^2 + 3 \rightarrow V = \$23.25$$

## Closing (5 minutes)

Read the bulleted statements to the class. Pause after each item, and ask students to offer examples of how the item was used in the last two lessons of this module. For example, after "specifying units," they may mention the units of the radiation half-life problem, or after "state the meaning of the symbols they choose," students may say, "In the business problems, we had to identify the expressions for profit, revenue, etc."

- Mathematically proficient students use clear definitions in discussion with others and in their own reasoning.
- They state the meaning of the symbols/variables they choose, including consistent and appropriate use of the equal sign.
- They are careful about specifying units of measure, and labeling axes to clarify the correspondence with quantities in a problem.
- They calculate accurately and efficiently, and express numerical answers with a degree of precision appropriate for the problem context.
- When given a verbal description, it is important to remember that functions used to model the relationships may have three representations: a table, an equation, or a graph.

---

**Lesson Summary**

The full modeling cycle is used to interpret the function and its graph, compute for the rate of change over an interval and attend to precision to solve real world problems in context of population growth and decay and other problems in geometric sequence or forms of linear, exponential, and quadratic functions.

---

## Exit Ticket (10 minutes)

Name _____    Date_____

# Lesson 9:  Modeling a Context From a Verbal Description

Exit Ticket

The distance a car travels before coming to a stop once a driver hits the brakes is related to the speed of the car when the brakes were applied.  The graph of $f$ (shown below) is a model of the stopping distance (in feet) of a car traveling at different speeds (in miles per hour).

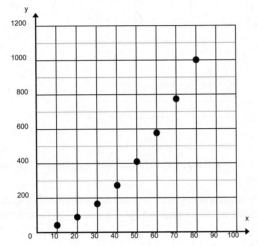

1.  One data point on the graph of $f$ appears to be (80,1000).  What do you think this point represents in the context of this problem.  Explain your reasoning.

2.  Estimate the stopping distance of the car if the driver is traveling at 65 mph when she hits the brakes.  Explain how you got your answer.

3.  Estimate the average rate of change of $f$ between $x = 50$ and $x = 60$.  What is the meaning of the rate of change in the context of this problem?

4.  What information would help you make a better prediction about stopping distance and average rate of change for this situation?

## Exit Ticket Sample Solutions

The distance a car travels before coming to a stop once a driver hits the brakes is related to the speed of the car when the brakes were applied. The graph of $f$ (shown) is a model of the stopping distance (in feet) of a car traveling at different speeds (in miles per hour).

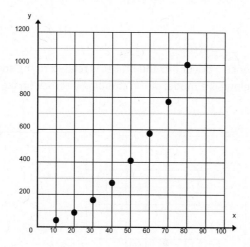

1.  One data point on the graph of $f$ appears to be $(80, 1000)$. What do you think this point represents in the context of this problem. Explain your reasoning.

    *In this problem, 80 would represent the speed in mph and 1000 would represent the stopping distance in feet. It doesn't make sense for a car to be traveling at 1000 mph, much less only take 80 feet to come to a stop.*

2.  Estimate the stopping distance of the car if the driver is traveling at 65 mph when she hits the brakes. Explain how you got your answer.

    *I can estimate the stopping distance by sketching a curve to connect the data points and locating the $y$-coordinate of a point on this curve when its $x$-coordinate is 65. My estimate is approximately 670 feet.*

    *Alternately, assume this is a quadratic function in the form $f(x) = kx^2$, where $f$ is the stopping distance, in feet, and $x$ is the speed, in miles per hour. Using the point $(80, 1000)$, $k = \frac{1000}{80^2} = 0.15625$ so $f(x) = 0.15625x^2$. Using this model, $f(65) = 660.15625$ mph.*

3.  Estimate the average rate of change of $f$ between $x = 50$ and $x = 60$. What is the meaning of the rate of change in the context of this problem?

    *$f(50) \approx 400$ and $f(60) \approx 580$. $\frac{580 - 400}{10} = 18$ ft./mph. This means that between 50 and 60 miles per hour the stopping distance is increasing by approximately 18 feet for each additional mph increase in speed.*

4.  What information would help you make a better prediction about stopping distance and average rate of change for this situation?

    *A table of data or an algebraic function would help in making better predictions.*

## Problem Set Sample Solutions

1. According to the Center for Disease and Control, the breast cancer rate for women has decreased at $0.9\%$ per year between 2000–2009.

   a. If $192,370$ women were diagnosed with invasive breast cancer in 2009, how many were diagnosed in 2005? For this problem, assume that the there is no change in population from 2005 and 2009.

      *Geometric Sequence:  common ratio is $(1 - 0.009) = 0.991$*

      $$a_n = a_1(common\ ratio)^{n-1}$$

      $$192,370 = a_1(0.991)^4$$

      $$192,370/(0.991)^4 = a_1$$

      $$a_1 = 199453.98 \dots$$

      $$a_1 = 199,454$$

   b. According to the American Cancer Society, in 2005 there were $211,240$ people diagnosed with breast cancer. In a written response, communicate how precise and accurate your solution in part (a) is, and explain why.

      *My solution is precise because my classmates and I followed the same protocols and our values were similar to each other.  Since the model we used did not take into account the population increase, our values were off by $11,786$ people which is $5.6\%$.  I believe that being off by only $5.6\%$ is still pretty close to the actual value.  My solution was precise and accurate; it could have been more accurate if the population growth was taken into account in the exponential model.*

2. The functions $f(x)$ and $g(x)$ represent the population of two different kinds of bacteria, where $x$ is the time (in hours) and $f(x)$ and $g(x)$ are the number of bacteria (in thousands).  $f(x) = 2x^2 + 7$ and $g(x) = 2^x$.

   a. Between the third and sixth hour, which bacteria had a faster rate of growth?

      *If you graph the functions, you can see that $g(x)$ is steeper between those two hours, and therefore has a faster rate of growth.*

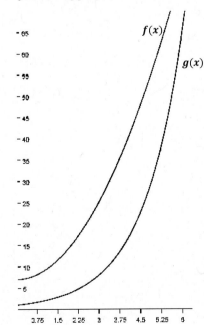

   *Using the functions to find the average rate of change over the interval $[3, 6]$, we have:*

   $$\frac{f(6) - f(3)}{6 - 3} = \frac{79 - 25}{3} = 18$$

   $$\frac{g(6) - g(3)}{6 - 3} = \frac{64 - 8}{3} \approx 18.7$$

   *$g(x)$ has a slightly higher average rate of change on this interval.*

b.    **Will the population of $g(x)$ ever exceed the population of $f(x)$? If so at what hour?**

*Since the question asks for the hour (not the exact time), I made a table starting at the 6th hour and compared the two functions. Once $g(x)$ exceeded $f(x)$, I stopped. So, sometime in the 7th hour, $g(x)$ exceeds $f(x)$.*

| Hour | $f(x)$ | $g(x)$ |
|------|--------|--------|
| 6    | 79     | 64     |
| 7    | 105    | 128    |

Name _____     Date _____

1.  In their entrepreneurship class, students are given two options for ways to earn a commission selling
    cookies.  For both options, students will be paid according to the number of boxes they are able to sell,
    with commissions being paid only after all sales have ended.  Students must commit to one commission
    option before they begin selling.

    Option 1:  The commission for each box of cookies sold is 2 dollars.
    Option 2:  The commission will be based on the total number of boxes of cookies sold as follows:  2 cents
    is the total commission if one box is sold, 4 cents is the commission if two boxes are sold, 8 cents if three
    boxes are sold, and so on, doubling the amount for each additional box sold.  (This option is based upon
    the total number of boxes sold and is paid on the total, not each individual box.)

    a.  Define the variables and write function equations to model each option.  Describe the domain for
        each function.

    b.  If Barbara thinks she can sell five boxes of cookies, should she choose Option 1 or 2?

    c.  Which option should she choose if she thinks she can sell ten boxes? Explain.

d. How many boxes of cookies would a student have to sell before Option 2 pays more than Option 1? Show your work and verify your answer graphically.

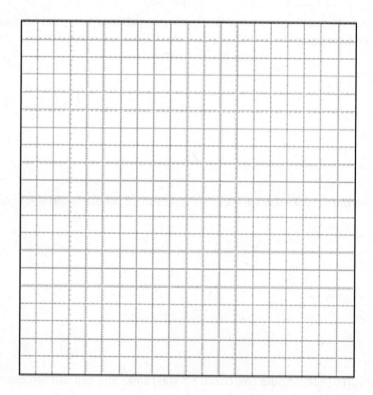

2. The table shows the average sale price $p$ of a house in New York City, for various years $t$ since 1960.

| Years since 1960, $t$ | 0 | 1 | 2 | 3 | 4 | 5 | 6 |
|---|---|---|---|---|---|---|---|
| Average sale price (in thousands of dollars), $p$ | 45 | 36 | 29 | 24 | 21 | 20 | 21 |

a. What type of function most appropriately represents this set of data? Explain your reasoning.

b. In what year is the price at the lowest? Explain how you know.

c. Write a function to represent the data. Show your work.

d. Can this function ever be equal to zero? Explain why or why not.

e. Mr. Samuels bought his house in New York City in 1970. If the trend continued, how much was he likely to have paid? Explain and provide mathematical evidence to support your answer.

3.  Veronica's physics class is analyzing the speed of a dropped object just before it hits the ground when it's dropped from different heights. They are comparing the final velocity, in feet/second, versus the height, in feet, from which the object was dropped. The class comes up with the following graph.

    a.  Use transformations of the parent function, $f(x) = \sqrt{x}$, to write an algebraic equation that represents this graph. Describe the domain in terms of the context.

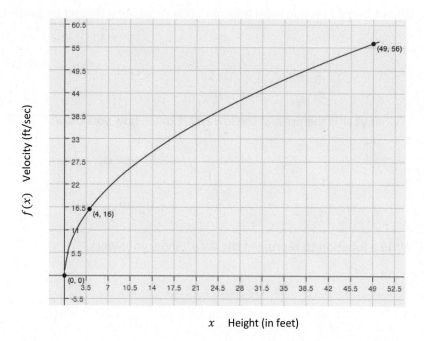

b.  Veronica and her friends are planning to go cliff diving at the end of the school year.  If she dives from a position that is 165 ft. above the water, at what velocity will her body be moving right before she enters the water?  Show your work and explain the level of precision you chose for your answer.

c.  Veronica's friend, Patrick, thinks that if she were able to dive from a 330-ft. position, she would experience a velocity that is twice as fast.  Is he correct?  Explain why or why not.

4.  Suppose that Peculiar Purples and Outrageous Oranges are two different and unusual types of bacteria. Both types multiply through a mechanism in which each single bacterial cell splits into four. However, they split at different rates: Peculiar Purples split every 12 minutes, while Outrageous Oranges split every 10 minutes.

    a.  If the multiplication rate remains constant throughout the hour and we start with three bacterial cells of each, after one hour, how many bacterial cells will there be of each type? Show your work and explain your answer.

    b.  If the multiplication rate remains constant for two hours, which type of bacteria is more abundant? What is the difference between the numbers of the two bacterial types after two hours?

    c.  Write a function to model the growth of Peculiar Purples and explain what the variable and parameters represent in the context.

d. Use your model from part (c) to determine how many Peculiar Purples there will be after three splits, i.e., at time 36 minutes. Do you believe your model has made an accurate prediction? Why or why not?

e. Write an expression to represent a different type of bacterial growth with an unknown initial quantity but in which each cell splits into 2 at each interval of time.

5. In a study of the activities of dolphins, a marine biologist made a slow-motion video of a dolphin swimming and jumping in the ocean with a specially equipped camera that recorded the dolphin's position with respect to the slow-motion time in seconds. Below is a piecewise quadratic graph, made from the slow-motion dolphin video, which represents a dolphin's vertical height (in feet, from the surface of the water) while swimming and jumping in the ocean, with respect to the slow-motion time (in seconds). Use the graph to answer the questions. [Note: The numbers in this graph are not necessarily real numbers from an actual dolphin in the ocean.]

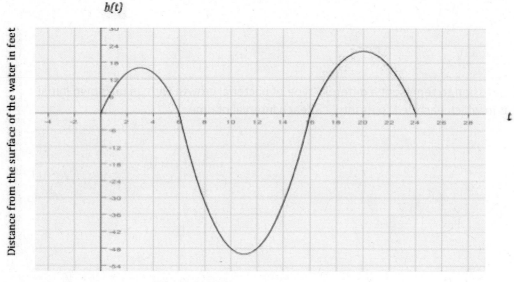

a. Given the vertex (11, – 50), write a function to represent the piece of the graph where the dolphin is underwater. Identify your variables and define the domain and range for your function.

b. Calculate the average rate of change for the interval from 6 to 8 seconds. Show your work and explain what your answer means in the context of this problem.

c.  Calculate the average rate of change for the interval from 14 to 16 seconds. Show your work and explain what your answer means in the context of this problem.

d.  Compare your answers for parts (b) and (c). Explain why the rates of change are different in the context of the problem.

6. The tables below represent values for two functions, *f* and *g*, one absolute value and one quadratic.

   a. Label each function as either <u>absolute value</u> or <u>quadratic</u>. Then explain mathematically how you identified each type of function.

   *f(x):* _____

   | x | f(x) |
   |---|---|
   | −3 | 1.5 |
   | −2 | 1 |
   | −1 | 0.5 |
   | 0 | 0 |
   | 1 | 0.5 |
   | 2 | 1 |
   | 3 | 1.5 |

   *g(x):* _____

   | x | g(x) |
   |---|---|
   | −3 | 4.5 |
   | −2 | 2 |
   | −1 | 0.5 |
   | 0 | 0 |
   | 1 | 0.5 |
   | 2 | 2 |
   | 3 | 4.5 |

   b. Represent each function graphically. Identify and label the key features of each in your graph (e.g., vertex, intercepts, axis of symmetry, etc.).

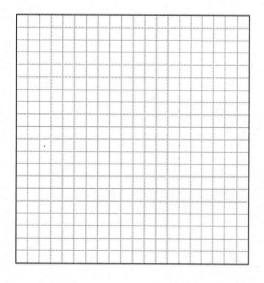
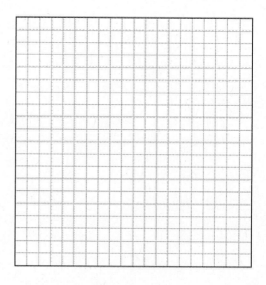

c. Represent each function algebraically.

7. Wendy won a one million dollar lottery! She will receive her winnings over the course of 10 years, which means she will get a check for $100,000 each year. In her college economics class, she learned about inflation, a general percentage increase in prices and fall in the purchasing power of money over time. (This is why prices from the past are sometimes referred to as "adjusted for inflation.") The inflation rate varies; from 2003 to 2013 the average rate has been 2.36% per year. This means that the value of a fixed dollar amount has decreased by 2.36%, on average, per year.

a. Wendy wants to make sure she gets the most out of her winnings, so she wants to figure out how much purchasing power she will lose over the course of the 10 years. Assume the average inflation rate will remain the same for the next 10 years. Complete the table below to help her calculate her losses in purchasing power due to inflation.

| Year | Check Amount | Purchasing Power After Adjusted for Inflation | Loss in Purchasing Power |
|------|--------------|-----------------------------------------------|--------------------------|
| 0 | 100,000.00 | 100,000.00 | 0.00 |
| 1 | 100,000.00 | 97,640.00 | 2,360.00 |
| 2 | 100,000.00 | | |
| 3 | 100,000.00 | | |
| 4 | 100,000.00 | | |
| 5 | 100,000.00 | | |
| 6 | 100,000.00 | | |
| 7 | 100,000.00 | | |
| 8 | 100,000.00 | | |
| 9 | 100,000.00 | | |
| 10 | 100,000.00 | | |

b. The far right column shows the estimated loss in purchasing power for each year based on 2.36% inflation. Wendy would like to know what her total loss in purchasing power will likely be. Taking into account that inflation varies each year and 2.36% represents the average inflation rate over a period of years, report an answer to Wendy. What will her total estimated loss be? Choose an appropriate level of accuracy and show or explain how you got your answer.

c.  James wrote the following equation to model this context: $P(t) = -2123.06t + 99612.56$.  Tiah wrote the equation: $Q(t) = 100{,}000(0.9764^t)$.  Which is a better model?  Explain why.

d.  Wendy decides to try to offset the effects of inflation by investing $50,000, from her first check only, in a mutual fund with an annual 5% return.  If she lets this money grow (i.e., she makes no deposits or withdrawals) for 10 years, will she make up the loss in purchasing power over the full 10 years?

## A Progression Toward Mastery

| Assessment Task Item | | STEP 1 Missing or incorrect answer and little evidence of reasoning or application of mathematics to solve the problem. | STEP 2 Missing or incorrect answer but evidence of some reasoning or application of mathematics to solve the problem. | STEP 3 A correct answer with some evidence of reasoning or application of mathematics to solve the problem, OR an incorrect answer with substantial evidence of solid reasoning or application of mathematics to solve the problem. | STEP 4 A correct answer supported by substantial evidence of solid reasoning or application of mathematics to solve the problem. |
|---|---|---|---|---|---|
| 1 | a<br><br>N-Q.A.2<br>N-Q.A.3<br>A-CED.2<br>F-BF.A.1<br>F-LE.A.1<br>F-LE.A.2<br>F-IF.B.5 | The student was unable to responds OR provided a minimal attempt to answer the three parts of the question.<br><br>None of the three components is accurate or complete. | Two of the following three components are missing, only partially correct, or incorrect:<br>1. Variables/quantities are defined appropriately<br>2. The domain is described, including the need to use cents in Option 2 and dollars in Option1<br>3. Both equations are accurately created<br>[Note: Only one of the three is accurate and complete.] | One of the following three components is missing, only partially correct, or incorrect:<br>1. Variables/quantities are defined appropriately<br>2. The domain is described, including the need to use cents in Option 2 and dollars in Option1<br>3. Both equations are accurately created<br>[Note: Two of the three are accurate and complete.] | Variables for the commission and the number of boxes sold are selected and defined appropriately. The domain issues are addressed (cents are used for one domain and dollars for the other). Accurate function equations are created using the defined quantities. |
| | b–c<br><br>N-Q.A.3<br>F-IF.A.4 | There was little or no attempt to answer these questions.<br><br>The answers were attempted but incorrect. | The student was able to answer the questions. The work was missing or partially supportive and the explanation was missing. | The student performed calculations correctly with accurate work shown and was able to answer the questions. The explanation was attempted but was incomplete or unclear. | The student answered the questions correctly, with accurate work shown, and with an appropriate level of precision, using cents or decimals for Option 2 and dollars for Option 1. The explanation was clear and complete. |

| | | | | | |
|---|---|---|---|---|---|
| | **d**<br><br>F-IF.B.4 | The answer is incorrect and there is no recognition of that fact as the student attempts to support the answer mathematically and graphically.<br><u>OR</u><br>There is little or no response to this question. | The student answers correctly that at 12 boxes Option 2 pays more than Option 1. There is little or no supporting mathematical or graphical reasoning. | The student answers correctly that at 12 boxes Option 2 pays more and some appropriate mathematical reasoning to support that answer is included – either tables, equations, <u>OR</u> graphs. However, the supporting work is only partially helpful. For example, the graph may be missing or does not show an understanding of the discrete nature of the data; the tables may not extend far enough to support the answer, <u>OR</u> the mathematical support may contain errors or be missing. | The student answers correctly that at 12 boxes Option 2 pays more and uses appropriate mathematical reasoning to support that answer (using tables or equations). The graph shows the discrete nature of the graphs, is accurately produced, and supports the answer. |
| **2** | **a**<br><br>F-IF.B.4 | The student misrepresents the function as something other than quadratic.<br><u>OR</u><br>There is no attempt made to answer this question. | The student correctly identifies the function as quadratic but provides no supporting evidence. | The student correctly identifies the function as quadratic and includes a partial, or partially accurate, explanation of rationale. | The student correctly identifies the function as quadratic and includes an accurate explanation of why the second differences are constant <u>OR</u> the pattern of the data shows a decrease and then an increase with varying average rates of change over the interval. The student may also include graphic support for the decision. |
| | **b, d**<br><br>F-IF.B.4 | There is no attempt made to answer this question. | The student attempts to interpret the data but answers the question incorrectly. Attempts at an explanation are not effective in highlighting the error. | The student accurately interprets the data to answer the question correctly. Explanations are only partially helpful or partially present. | The student accurately interprets the data to answer the question correctly. Explanations are accurate and complete and relate to the key feature being addressed (minimum value of the function and $x$-intercepts). |

| | | | | | |
|---|---|---|---|---|---|
| | **c**<br><br>A-CED.A.2<br>F-BF.A.1 | There is little or no attempt made to answer this question. | The student attempted to determine a quadratic equation but made computational errors that resulted in an incorrect function equation. | The student accurately arrives at the correct quadratic equation for this function. Supporting work is present, clear, and accurate. However, there is no evidence that the student considered the value of the leading coefficient. | The student accurately arrives at the correct quadratic equation for this function. Supporting work is present, clear, and accurate and includes determining the fact that the leading coefficient is 1. |
| | **e**<br><br>N-Q.A.3<br>F-IF.B.4 | The student provides an incorrect answer. OR<br><br>There is little or no attempt made to answer this question. | The student provides the correct response of $45,000, but provides no mathematical support or explanation of the solution.<br><br>OR the student correctly determines that 1970 is interpreted as t = 10 but makes an error in calculation that leads to an incorrect result. | The student accurately interprets the data to answer the question correctly. Results may not be reported with the correct level of precision: 1970 is interpreted as $t = 10$ and the final solution is given as $f(10) = 45$. The explanation may be partially effective: calculations or explanation missing or partially present. | The student accurately interprets the data to answer the question correctly. Results are reported with the correct level of precision: 1970 is interpreted as $t = 10$ and the final solution is given as $45,000 rather than $f(10) = 45$. Mathematical support includes accurate calculations. |
| **3** | **a**<br><br>A-CED.A.1<br>A.CED.A.2<br>F-IF.B.5<br>F-BF.A.1 | The student does not recognize the graph as representing a square-root function.<br>OR<br>There is little or no attempt to answer this question. | The student recognizes that the graph is a square root function and presents the correct parent function: $f(x) = \sqrt{x}$. However, there is no attempt or an incorrect method is used to find the specific function. A 1-variable equation that would be used to find the function equation is either missing or ineffective. The student may or may not have domain restrictions correctly described for this rating level. | The student correctly interprets the graph to represent a square root function with parent of $f(x) = \sqrt{x}$, and accurately uses algebraic manipulation to solve the 1-variable equation that indicates that the function equation is $f(x) = 8\sqrt{x}$. However, restrictions on the domain $\{x \geq 0\}$, are either not present, incorrect, or are missing information about the need for one interval to be open at 0.<br>OR<br>The graph is correctly interpreted as a square root function and an attempt is made to determine the function, | The student correctly does all three parts of this question:<br>1. Interprets the graph to represent a square root function with parent of $f(x) = \sqrt{x}$.<br>2. Accurately determines that the function is stretched and uses correct algebraic manipulation to solve the 1-variable equation that indicates that the function equation is $f(x) = 8\sqrt{x}$.<br>3. Restrictions on the domain $\{x \geq 0\}$, are present either symbolically or as part of the explanation. Some |

| | | | | but an error in calculation resulted in an incorrect result. Domain restrictions are accurately described. | understanding of the limitations on the domain in the context should be apparent. |
|---|---|---|---|---|---|
| **b**<br><br>N-Q.A.3<br>F-IF.B.4 | There is little or no attempt to answer this question. | The student attempts to interpret the problem situation but does not use the correct function value, $f(165)$ and/or makes calculation errors that lead to an incorrect answer. | The student accurately interprets the problem situation and correctly uses an incorrect equation (finds $f(165)$ from part (a)). Even though they are not accurate, results are reported with the correct level of precision. | The student accurately interprets the problem situation to answer the question correctly. Results are reported with the correct level of precision: ($8\sqrt{165}$ or 102.3 ft/sec) |
| **c**<br><br>N-Q.A.3<br>F-IF.B.4 | There is little or no attempt to answer this question.<br>__OR__<br>The student agrees with Patrick. | The student attempts to interpret the problem situation but does not use the correct function value, $f(330)$ and/or makes calculation errors that lead to an incorrect answer. They agree with Veronica but there is no clear or valid explanation of the reasoning behind the agreement. | The student accurately interprets the problem situation and correctly uses an incorrect equation (finds $f(330)$ $- 8\sqrt{330}$ or 102 ft./sec). The explanation includes agreement with Veronica but does not include supporting argument involving the key features of a square root function as compared to a linear (Patrick's assumption).<br>__OR__<br>The student accurately interprets the problem situation to answer the question correctly ($8\sqrt{330}$ or 102 ft./sec) but provides no explanation of their reasoning. | The student accurately interprets the problem situation to answer the question correctly ($8\sqrt{330}$ or 102 ft./sec). They explanation includes agreement with Veronica and describes the key features of a square root function as it relates to a linear function (Patrick's assumption). |
| **4** **a–b**<br><br>N-Q.A.2<br>N-Q.A.3<br>F-LE.A.1 | There is little or no attempt to answer this question. | The student defines the quantities and the variables in the problem but makes calculation errors that lead to an incorrect answer. There is inadequate explanation of the process and/or the relationship between the number of splits per | The student defines the quantities and the variables in the problem and calculates correctly to find the number of cells after one hour for each type of bacteria (Orange is 12,288, Purple is 3,072). There is partial evidence of the required work | The student defines the quantities and the variables in the problem and calculates correctly to find the number of cells after one hour for each type of bacteria (Orange is 12,288, Purple is 3,072). The work is shown and supports the correct |

Module 5:    A Synthesis of Modeling with Equations and Functions
Date:        10/4/13

| | | hour and the growth of the two bacteria types. | and/or the answers are not adequately explained. Answers are given with the appropriate attention to precision. Part (b) might be given exactly but may be rounded at this level (i.e., answers might be given to three significant digits: 50.3 million for Oranges and 3.15 million for Purples and the difference: 47.2 million – or they may be appropriately rounded to the nearest million.) | answers found. The explanation incudes the fact that the two types of bacterial have a different number of divisions in the hour, so one is growing faster than the other, even though both are splitting in the same way (into four). Answers are given with the appropriate attention to precision. Part (b) might be given exactly but may be rounded for full credit (i.e., answers might be given to three significant digits: 50.3 million for Oranges and 3.15 million for Purples and the difference: 47.2 million – or they may be appropriately rounded to the nearest million.) |
|---|---|---|---|---|
| **c–d**<br><br>**N-Q.A.2**<br>**A-CED.A.2**<br>**F-LE.A.2** | There is little or no attempt to answer this question. | The student attempts to use the described situation to create a 2-variable equation but does not clearly understand how the exponential function should be formed. Errors are made in forming the function equation and/or parameters are missing or incorrect. | The student attempts to use the described situation to create a 2-variable exponential equation but is missing one or more of the parameters and/or does not attend to the leading coefficient of the exponential expression. | The student uses correctly defined variables to create a 2-variable exponential equation that fits the described situation. All parameters are correctly represented. |
| **5**    **a**<br><br>**N-Q.A.2**<br>**A.CED.A.2**<br>**F-IF.B.5** | An incorrect method is attempted to find a quadratic equation.<br>OR<br>There is little or no attempt to answer this question. | There is an attempt to create a 2-variable quadratic equation. However, the values used are incorrect or are used incorrectly, leading to an incorrect equation. There is no attention paid to the leading coefficient, and the domain and range explanations are missing. | The student creates a 2-variable equation based on the correct section of the graph, using the given vertex coordinates. Student correctly computes to find the leading coefficient, leading to the correct function equation: $h(t) = 2(x-11)^2 - 50$. The domain and range | The student creates a 2-variable equation based on the correct section of the graph, using the given vertex coordinates. Student also correctly computes to find the leading coefficient, leading to the correct function equation: $h(t) = 2(x-11)^2 - 50$. The explanation of the |

Module 5:     A Synthesis of Modeling with Equations and Functions
Date:         10/4/13

138

| | | | | explanations are missing, inadequate, or incorrect. | domain $[6, 16]$ and range $[0, -50]$ are clear and accurate. |
|---|---|---|---|---|---|
| | **b–c**<br><br>F-IF.B.4<br>F-IF.B.6 | There is little or no attempt to answer this question. | The student attempts to find the average rate of change but errors in calculation lead to incorrect answers. Explanations are missing or ineffective. | The student calculates the rate of change and shows all work but does not adequately explain what the rates mean in terms of the context. | The student accurately calculates the average rate of change over the indicated intervals, with all necessary work shown. Student explains the answer in terms of the rate of speed for the dolphin and the direction it is moving. |
| | **d**<br><br>F-IF.B.4<br>F-IF.B.6 | There is little or no attempt to answer this question. | The student attempts to compare the two average rates of change but is unable to identify the similarities or differences or make a connection to the context. | The student recognizes that the two average rates of change are opposites but does not adequately explain the connection to the context. | The student explains how and why, in terms of the context, the two average rates are different. |
| **6** | **a**<br><br>F-BF.A.1 | There is little or no attempt to answer this question. | The student correctly identifies one of the two functions and correctly explains how the correct one is determined. The other is incorrectly identified and the explanation is missing or ineffective. | The student correctly identifies the function for each table of values and accurately and clearly explains how they arrived at their conclusion. The accompanying explanation does not include average rates of change of different intervals for $f(x)$ being constant and varying for $g(x)$. | The student correctly identifies the function for each table of values and accurately and clearly explains how they arrived at their conclusion. The explanation includes average rates of change of different intervals for $f(x)$ being constant and varying for $g(x)$. |
| | **b**<br><br>F-BF.A.1 | There is little or no attempt to answer this question. | The student graphs only one of the two functions correctly and identifies/labels the key features. The graphs may or may not have scales the axes labeled. | The student graphs both functions correctly but does not identify or label the key features. The graphs are clear and have the scale and the axes labeled. | The student accurately creates the graphs for both functions with labels for the vertices and the axes of symmetry. The graphs are clear and have the scale and the axes labeled. |

| | | | | | |
|---|---|---|---|---|---|
| | **c**<br><br>A-CED.A.2<br>F-IF.B.6 | There is little or no attempt to answer this question. | The student accurately creates one of the two functions correctly with work shown. If the equation for $f(x)$ is accurately completed, there should be evidence of understanding that 0 is not in the domain for both intervals in the piecewise defined function. [One or the other of the intervals must have an open endpoint at 0.] Supporting work is shown for the correct equation. The other may be incomplete or incorrect. | The student accurately creates the absolute value function either in absolute value form $(f(x) = \frac{1}{2}|x|)$ or as a piecewise defined function: $(f(x) = \frac{1}{2}x$ for $0 \le x \le +\infty$; and $f(x) = -\frac{1}{2}x$ for $-\infty \le x \le 0.)$ There is no indication that the student understands that 0 is not in the domain for both intervals in the piecewise defined function. [Note: One or the other of the intervals must have an open endpoint at 0.] The second is correctly identified as $g(x) = \frac{1}{2}x^2$. Work is shown that supports the correct answers. | The student accurately creates the absolute value function either in absolute value form $(f(x) = \frac{1}{2}|x|)$ or as a piecewise defined function: $(f(x) = \frac{1}{2}x$ for $0 < x < +\infty$; and $f(x) = -\frac{1}{2}x$ for $-\infty < x < 0.)$ [Note: It should be clear that 0 is not in the domain for both intervals in the piecewise defined function. One or the other of the intervals must have an open endpoint at 0.]] The second is correctly identified as $g(x) = \frac{1}{2}x^2$. Work is shown that supports the correct answers. |
| **7.** | **a**<br><br>N-Q.A.3 | There is little or no attempt to answer this question. | The table of values is partially completed and partially correct (3 or more calculations are missing or incorrect). | The table of values is completely filled in with only one or two errors in calculation. <u>OR</u> Decimal approximations are consistently imprecise with all calculations correctly completed.<br><br>An explanation might be included but is not required. If included, all statements are accurate and precise. | The table of values is completed correctly with appropriate decimal approximations. An explanation might be included but is not required. If included, all statements are accurate and precise. |
| | **b**<br><br>N-Q.A.3 | There is no attempt to answer this question. | The student attempted to use the values from the far right column of their table for part (a). However there are calculation errors or a lack of understanding about what the calculations to perform and why. | The student correctly explains or shows to be adding all the values in the far right column. A calculation error was made so that the final answer was not correct and/or the rounding was incorrect, with values not rounded | The correct answer is given as $120,000 or $121,000 or other justified estimate. Note that reporting as $121,029.92 does not take into account the fact that we are working with a model based on an approximation. All |

Module 5:   A Synthesis of Modeling with Equations and Functions
Date:        10/4/13

| | | | | | |
|---|---|---|---|---|---|
| | | | | appropriately. For example, reporting the answer as $121,029.92 does not take into account the fact that we are using a model based on approximations. [Note: This answer is dependent on the values found in part (a). Students using incorrect values correctly in part (b) should receive full credit for part (b).] | values in the table and the answer may be rounded to the nearest whole dollar but also appropriately rounded for currency to the 0.01. [Note: This answer is dependent on the values found in part (a). Students using incorrect values correctly in part (b) should receive full credit for part (b).] |
| **c** N-Q.A.3 A.CED.A.2 F-BF.A.1 F.LE.A.1 | There is little or no attempt to answer this question. | The student attempts to explain the limitations of the model but does not clarify that the model is linear or that it will descend into negative values over the long run. | The explanation shows recognition that the function James has chosen is linear but is not clear as to why it will not be a good model in the long run (descends into negative values). | The explanation includes information about the function James is using being linear. (The correlation coefficient for the linear model is $-0.9994$ so it is clearly a good model for this domain.) The student points out that after a longer period of time the linear function will descend into the negatives, which is not reasonable for this context. An explanation of the preferred exponential function might be included, but is not required. |
| **d** N-Q.A.3 A.CED.A.2 | There is little or no attempt to answer this question. | The student uses the correct formula for exponential growth, $C(t) = P(1 + r)^t$, but is not able to substitute the correct values from the prompt for the initial investment, the rate, and the time. Consequently, calculations are incorrect. | The student uses the correct formula for exponential growth, $C(t) = P(1 + r)^t$ and accurately substitutes values for initial investment, rate, and time. There are errors in calculation or rounding that offer a solution other than $81,444.73. The student is able to subtract the original $50,000 from the earnings found and gives the answer: NO, | The student uses the correct formula for exponential growth, $C(t) = 50,000(1.05)^{10}$ and accurately calculates the earnings to be $81,444.73. The student then subtracts the original $50,000 to find that the earnings will be $31,444.73 and answers: NO, this is not even half of the purchasing power she will lose over the course of the 10 years. |

| | | | | this is not enough interest to offset the loss of purchasing power she will incur over the course of the 10 years. | |
|---|---|---|---|---|---|

Name _____     Date _____

1.  In their entrepreneurship class, students are given two options for ways to earn a commission selling cookies.  For both options, students will be paid according to the number of boxes they are able to sell, with commissions being paid only after all sales have ended.  Students must commit to one commission option before they begin selling.

    Option 1:  The commission for each box of cookies sold is 2 dollars.
    Option 2:  The commission will be based on the total number of boxes of cookies sold as follows:  2 cents is the total commission if one box is sold, 4 cents is the commission if two boxes are sold, 8 cents if three boxes are sold, and so on, doubling the amount for each additional box sold.  (This option is based upon the total number of boxes sold and is paid on the total, not each individual box.)

    a.  Define the variables and write function equations to model each option.  Describe the domain for each function.

    *Let C represent the commission for each option in dollars for Option 1 and in cents for Option 2. [Note: students may try to use .02 for the exponential base but will find that the decimals present problems. They might also use 200 for Option 1 so that both can use cents as the unit. However as long as they are careful they can use different units for each function.]*

    *Let x represent the number of boxes sold.*

    $C_1 = 2x$        *(in dollars)*

    $C_2 = 2^x$        *(in cents)*

    *Domain: Positive integers.*

    b.  If Barbara thinks she can sell five boxes of cookies, should she choose Option 1 or 2?

    *5 boxes:*        *Option 1 – $C_1 = 2(5) = \underline{\$10}$*

    *Option 2 – $C_2 = 2^5 = \underline{32¢\ or\ \$.32}$*

    *She should choose Option 1 because she will make more money.*

    c.  Which option should she choose if she thinks she can sell ten boxes? Explain.

    *10 boxes:*     *Option 1 – $C_1 = 2(10) = \underline{\$20}$*

    *Option 2 – $C_2 = 2^{10} = \underline{1024¢\ or\ \$10.24}$*

    *She should still choose Option 1 because the commission is still higher.*

d. How many boxes of cookies would a student have to sell before Option 2 pays more than Option 1? Show your work and verify your answer graphically.

Using tables: We see that at 11 boxes Option 1 is still more than Option 2 but after that it reverses.

| x (boxes) | C1 (dollars) |
|-----------|--------------|
| 1 | 2 |
| 2 | 4 |
| 3 | 6 |
| 5 | 10 |
| 10 | 20 |
| 11 | 22 |
| 12 | 24 |

| x (boxes) | C2 (cents) |
|-----------|------------|
| 1 | 0.02 |
| 2 | 0.04 |
| 3 | 0.06 |
| 5 | 0.10 |
| 10 | 10.24 |
| 11 | 20.48 |
| 12 | 40.96 |

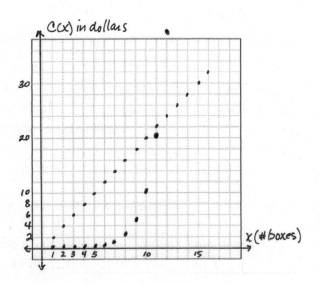

When graphing both functions on the same coordinate plane it is important to remember to use the same units for both equations and that the graph will be discrete.

2. The table shows the average sale price $p$ of a house in New York City, for various years $t$ since 1960.

| Years since 1960, $t$ | 0 | 1 | 2 | 3 | 4 | 5 | 6 |
|---|---|---|---|---|---|---|---|
| Average sale price (in thousands of dollars), $p$ | 45 | 36 | 29 | 24 | 21 | 20 | 21 |

a. What type of function most appropriately represents this set of data? Explain your reasoning.

   <u>Quadratic</u> – The first differences are not the same but the second differences are.

b. In what year is the price at the lowest? Explain how you know.

   The lowest price was when $t = 5$ or <u>1965</u>. The lowest price in the data set is $20,000 – this is the vertex/minimum.

c. Write a function to represent the data. Show your work.

   We use the general vertex form: $f(t) = a(t - h)^2 + k$ ...

   $f(t) = a(t - 5)^2 + 20$

   Substituting an ordered pair we know, $(0, 45)$ we get:

   $45 = a(-5)^2 + 20$  ...  $45 = 25a + 20$  ...  $25 = 25a$  SO  $a = 1$

   <u>$f(t) = (x - 5)^2 + 20$</u>

d. Can this function ever be equal to zero? Explain why or why not.

   No, The lowest price is at the vertex: $20,000.

e. Mr. Samuels bought his house in New York City in 1970. If the trend continued, how much was he likely to have paid? Explain and provide mathematical evidence to support your answer.

   1970 would be when $t = 10$. If we substitute 10 into the function equation in part c we get: $f(10) = (5)^2 + 20 = 25 + 20 = 45$. So he would have paid $45,000 for his house.

3.  Veronica's physics class is analyzing the speed of a dropped object just before it hits the ground when it's dropped from different heights.  They are comparing the final velocity, in feet/second, versus the height, in feet, from which the object was dropped.  The class comes up with the following graph.

a.  Use transformations of the parent function, $f(x) = \sqrt{x}$, to write an algebraic equation that represents this graph.  Describe the domain in terms of the context.

The graph represents a square root function. The parent function of the square root function is f(x) = √x.  From the image of the graph I can tell the graph hasn't shifted left or right but from the points given it has been stretched.  I will use the point (4,16) to find the symbolic representation of the graph and then use the point (49, 56) to check that my function is correct.  The domain is the set of all real numbers greater than or equal to 0. However realistically there is a limit to how big the numbers can go since there are limits

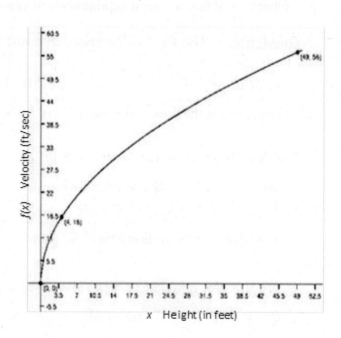

f(x) = √(ax) → 16 = √(a4) → 16 = 2√a → 16/2 = √a → 8 = √a → 64 = a [Note: starting with f(x) = a √x, will reach the same end result.]

Check:

f(x) = √64x → f(x) = 8√x → 56 = 8√49 → 56 = 8(7) → 56 = 56 ✓   <u>f(x) = 8√x  (x ≥ 0)</u>

b.   Veronica and her friends are planning to go cliff diving at the end of the school year. If she dives from a position that is 165 ft. above the water, at what velocity will her body be moving right before she enters the water? Show your work and explain the level of precision you chose for your answer.

$f(165) = 8\sqrt{165} \approx 102.8$ ft/sec or **103 ft/sec**. Since the information in the problem is given to the nearest whole number of feet and seconds, I decided to do the same for my answer.

c.   Veronica's friend, Patrick, thinks that if she were able to dive from a 330-ft. position, she would experience a velocity that is twice as fast. Is he correct? Explain why or why not.

He is not correct. Patrick is describing the relationship between the velocity and the height as if it was a linear function but it isn't. The graph that represents the relationship between the two is a square root, which has average rates of change on different intervals that is different from a linear function. I rounded to the nearest whole number because this is a model and only approximates a real-world phenomenon.

$f(330) = 8\sqrt{330} \rightarrow = 145.3$ or **145 ft/sec** which is not double the 102 ft/sec speed calculated before.

4. Suppose that Peculiar Purples and Outrageous Oranges are two different and unusual types of bacteria. Both types multiply through a mechanism in which each single bacterial cell splits into four. However, they split at different rates: Peculiar Purples split every 12 minutes, while Outrageous Oranges split every 10 minutes.

   a. If the multiplication rate remains constant throughout the hour and we start with three bacterial cells of each, after one hour, how many bacterial cells will there be of each type? Show your work and explain your answer.

Let n = the number of 10-minute or 12-minute time intervals. Then P (n) represents the number of

purples and O (n) represents the number of Oranges at the end of any time period. The tables below

show the number of bacterial cells after 1 hour for each:

| n | P (n) |
|---|---|
| 0 | 3 |
| 1 (12 min) | 12 |
| 2 (24 min) | 48 |
| 3 (36 min) | 192 |
| 4 (48 min) | 768 |
| 5 (60 min) | 3072 |

| n | O (n) |
|---|---|
| 0 | 3 |
| 1 (10 min) | 12 |
| 2 (20 min) | 48 |
| 3 (30 min) | 192 |
| 4 (50 min) | 768 |
| 5 (50 min) | 3072 |
| 6 (60 min) | 12,288 |

   b. If the multiplication rate remains constant for two hours, which type of bacteria is more abundant? What is the difference between the numbers of the two bacterial types after two hours?

Continuing the table from part (a) we find that the Oranges will have one more split in

the first hour so two more in the second. The Oranges will have 47,185,920 more

bacterial cells than the Purples. (At 2 hours Oranges = 50,331,648 and Purples =

3,145,728

   c. Write a function to model the growth of Peculiar Purples and explain what the variable and parameters represent in the context.

P (n) = 3 (4ⁿ), where n represents the number of 12-minute splits, 3 is the initial

value, and 4 is the number of Purples created for each split.

d.  Use your model from part (c) to determine how many Peculiar Purples there will be after three splits, i.e., at time 36 minutes.  Do you believe your model has made an accurate prediction?  Why or why not?

$P(3) = 3(4^3) = 3(64) = 192.$  Yes, this matches the values I found in the table for part (a).

e.  Write an expression to represent a different type of bacterial growth with an unknown initial quantity but in which each cell splits into 2 at each interval of time.

$F(n) = a(2^n)$, where n represents the number of time interval and a represents the initial number of bacterial cells.

5.  In a study of the activities of dolphins, a marine biologist made a slow-motion video of a dolphin swimming and jumping in the ocean with a specially equipped camera that recorded the dolphin's position with respect to the slow-motion time in seconds.  Below is a piecewise quadratic graph, made from the slow-motion dolphin video, which represents a dolphin's vertical height (in feet, from the surface of the water) while swimming and jumping in the ocean, with respect to the slow-motion time (in seconds).  Use the graph to answer the questions.  [Note: The numbers in this graph are not necessarily real numbers from an actual dolphin in the ocean.]

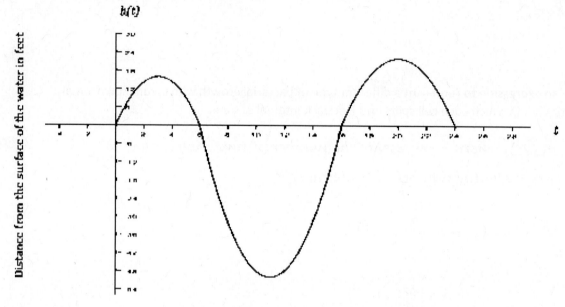

a.  Given the vertex $(11, -50)$, write a function to represent the piece of the graph where the dolphin is underwater.  Identify your variables and define the domain and range for your function.

*Using the vertex form for a quadratic function equation: $h(t) = a(t - h)^2 + k$, we know the*

*vertex $(h, K)$ to be $(11, -50)$. Now to find the leading coefficient, we can substitute a point we*

*know, say $(6, 0)$, and solve for a:*

$0 = a(6 - 11)^2 - 50 \ldots a(-5)^2 = 50 \ldots 25a = 50 \ldots a = 2$

*SO: $\underline{h(t) = 2(t - 11)^2 - 50}$*

*Domain (interval of time in seconds): $[6, 16]$*

*Range (distance from the surface): $[0, -50]$*

b.  Calculate the average rate of change for the interval from 6 to 8 seconds.  Show your work and explain what your answer means in the context of this problem.

*Average rate of change: $[h(8) - h(6)] / (8 - 6) = (-32 - 0) / 2 = -16$*

*The dolphin is moving downward at an average rate of 16 feet per second.*

c. Calculate the average rate of change for the interval from 14 to 16 seconds. Show your work and explain what your answer means in the context of this problem.

Average rate of change: $[h(16) - h(14)] / (16 - 14) = (0 - -32) / 2 = +16$

The dolphin is moving upward at a rate of 16 feet per second.

d. Compare your answers for parts (b) and (c). Explain why the rates of change are different in the context of the problem.

The two average rates show that the dolphin's rate is the same for each interval except that in the first it is moving downward and in the second upward. They are different because of the symmetric nature of the quadratic graph. The intervals chosen are symmetric so will have the same y-values.

6.  The tables below represent values for two functions, *f* and *g*, one absolute value and one quadratic.

a.  Label each function as either <u>absolute value</u> or <u>quadratic</u>.  Then explain mathematically how you identified each type of function.

*f(x):* <u>absolute value</u>          *g(x):* <u>quadratic</u>

| x | f(x) |
|---|------|
| −3 | 1.5 |
| −2 | 1 |
| −1 | .5 |
| 0 | 0 |
| 1 | .5 |
| 2 | 1 |
| 3 | 1.5 |

| x | g(x) |
|---|------|
| −3 | 4.5 |
| −2 | 2 |
| −1 | .5 |
| 0 | 0 |
| 1 | .5 |
| 2 | 2 |
| 3 | 4.5 |

In the first table [f (x)] the rates on any interval on the same side of the vertex (0, 0) is ½ and on the other side of the vertex the rates of change are all − ½.

In the second table [g (x)] the rates vary on each side of the vertex: The intervals closest to the vertex have average rates of ½ and − ½ but the next intervals have −1.5 and +1.5, then −2.5 and +2.5, etc.

For this reason the first is absolute value (linear piecewise) and the second is quadratic.

b.  Represent each function graphically.  Identify and label the key features of each in your graph (e.g., vertex, intercepts, axis of symmetry, etc.).

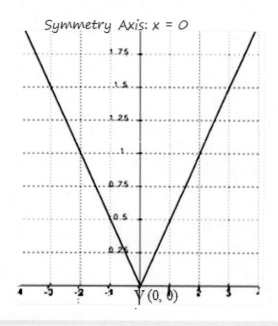

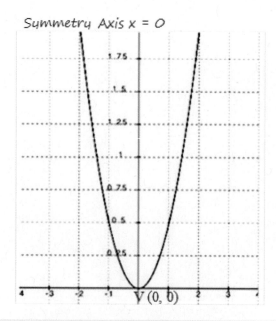

c.  Represent each function algebraically.

$$f(x) = \tfrac{1}{2}\,|x| \quad \text{OR} \quad f(x) = \begin{cases} \dfrac{1}{2}x, & 0 \le x \\[2mm] -\dfrac{1}{2}x, & -\infty < x < 0 \end{cases}$$

$g(x) = a(x - h)^2 + k$ with $V(0, 0)$

So: $g(x) = ax^2$

Substituting an ordered pair we know, $(2, 2)$:

$2 = a(2)^2$

$a = \tfrac{1}{2}$

SO: $\underline{g(x) = \tfrac{1}{2}\,x^2}$

[NOTE: Since it is obvious that the quadratic function is not translated the equation could be found by using $y = ax^2$ in the first step.]

7. Wendy won a one million dollar lottery! She will receive her winnings over the course of 10 years, which means she will get a check for $100,000 each year. In her college economics class, she learned about inflation, a general percentage increase in prices and fall in the purchasing power of money over time. (This is why prices from the past are sometimes referred to as "adjusted for inflation.") The inflation rate varies; from 2003 to 2013 the average rate has been 2.36% per year. This means that the value of a fixed dollar amount has decreased by 2.36%, on average, per year.

a. Wendy wants to make sure she gets the most out of her winnings, so she wants to figure out how much purchasing power she will lose over the course of the 10 years. Assume the average inflation rate will remain the same for the next 10 years. Complete the table below to help her calculate her losses in purchasing power due to inflation.

| Year | Check Amount | Purchasing Power After Adjusted for Inflation | Loss in Purchasing Power |
|------|--------------|-----------------------------------------------|--------------------------|
| 0 | 100,000.00 | 100,000.00 | 0.00 |
| 1 | 100,000.00 | 97,640.00 | 2,360.00 |
| 2 | 100,000.00 | 95,335.70 | 4,663.30 |
| 3 | 100,000.00 | 93,085.77 | 6,914.23 |
| 4 | 100,000.00 | 90,888.95 | 9,111.05 |
| 5 | 100,000.00 | 88,743.97 | 11,256.03 |
| 6 | 100,000.00 | 86,649.61 | 13,350.39 |
| 7 | 100,000.00 | 84,604.68 | 15,395.32 |
| 8 | 100,000.00 | 82,608.01 | 17,391.99 |
| 9 | 100,000.00 | 80,658.46 | 19,341.54 |
| 10 | 100,000.00 | 78,754.92 | 21,245.08 |

[Note: Students may use the analytical model, $C(t) = P(1 - r)^t = P(1 - 0.0236)^t$, to calculate the value of the money with P representing the initial value, r the inflation rate, and t the time in years. However the data table on its own is an adequate model for this small and discrete domain.]

b. The far right column shows the estimated loss in purchasing power for each year based on 2.36% inflation. Wendy would like to know what her total loss in purchasing power will likely be. Taking into account that inflation varies each year and 2.36% represents the average inflation rate over a period of years, report an answer to Wendy. What will her total estimated loss be? Choose an appropriate level of accuracy and show or explain how you got your answer.

*If we add up the losses in purchasing power of each year's payment we see that in 10 years Wendy is likely to lose about $121,030 in purchasing power over time at the present average yearly inflation rate.*

c.   James wrote the following equation to model this context: $P(t) = -2123.06t + 99612.56$.  Tiah wrote the equation: $Q(t) = 100{,}000(0.9764^t)$. Which is a better model? Explain why.

*For the domain of this context both a linear and exponential function can provide good models, with the exponential being slightly better. [Correlation coefficient for the linear regression is –0.9994 and for the exponential regression it is –1.] The exponential model is best over longer periods of time, as the linear function will eventually become negative and this will not happen with the inflation rates. For the exponential model the value of the money will level off and approach zero over longer periods of time, which is what we would expect for inflation rates.*

d.   Wendy decides to try to offset the effects of inflation by investing $50,000, from her first check only, in a mutual fund with an annual 5% return.  If she lets this money grow (i.e., she makes no deposits or withdrawals) for 10 years, will she make up the loss in purchasing power over the full 10 years?

*Sample solution:*

$C(t) = P(1+r)^t$

$C(10) = 50{,}000(1.05)^{10} = \$81{,}444.73$

*She will earn about $31,444.73, which is not even half of the purchasing power she will lose during that time period (10 years). She needs to invest more initially or invest more over time.*

# Mathematics Curriculum

# Student Materials

# Lesson 1:  Analyzing a Graph

Classwork

**Opening Exercise**

The graphs below give examples for each parent function we have studied this year.  For each graph, identify the function type, and the general form of the parent function's equation; then offer general observations on the key features of the graph that helped you identify the function type. (Function types include:  linear, quadratic, exponential, square root, cube root, cubic, absolute value, and other piecewise functions.  Key features may include the overall shape of the graph, $x$- and $y$-intercepts, symmetry, a vertex, end behavior, domain and range values/restrictions, and average rates of change over an interval.)

| FUNCTION SUMMARY CHART | | |
| --- | --- | --- |
| **Graph** | **Function Type and Parent Function** | **Function Clues:  Key Features, observations** |
| | | |
| | | |

Lesson 1:       Analyzing a Graph
Date:            9/24/13

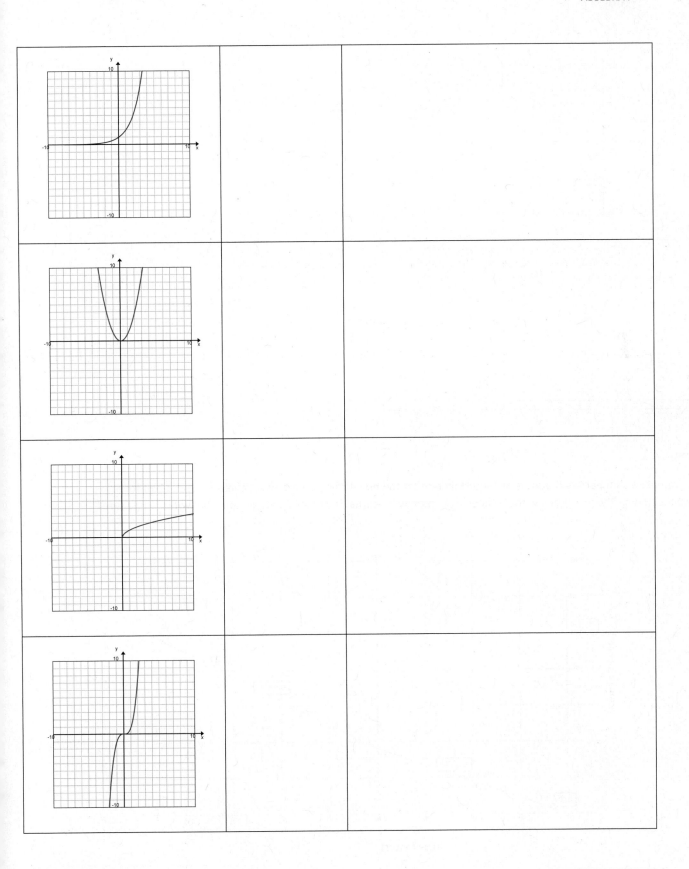

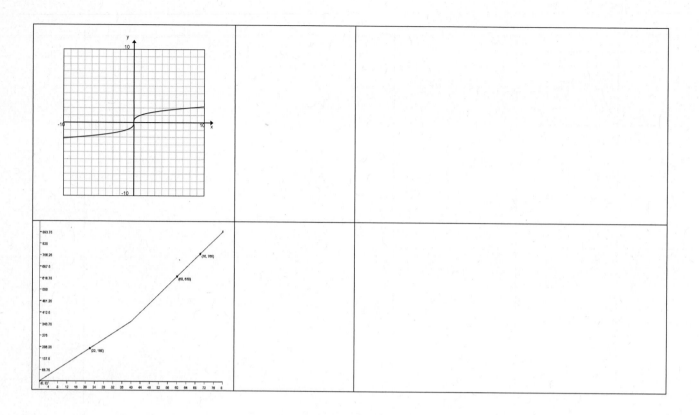

## Example 1

Eduardo has a summer job that pays him a certain rate for the first 40 hours each week and time-and-a-half for any overtime hours.  The graph below shows how much money he earns as a function of the hours he works in one week.

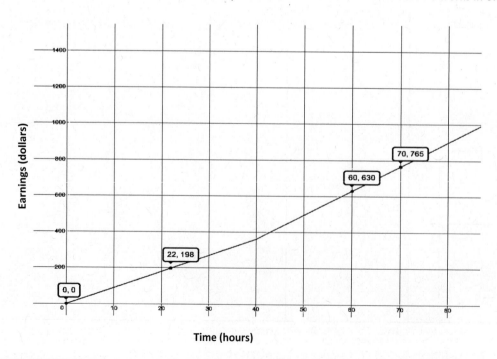

**Time (hours)**

**Exercises**

1.  Write the function in analytical (symbolic) form for the graph in Example 1.

    a.  What is the equation for the first piece of the graph?

    b.  What is the equation for the second piece of the graph?

    c.  What are the domain restrictions for the context?

    d.  Explain the domain in the context of the problem.

For each graph below use the questions and identified ordered pairs to help you formulate an equation to represent it.

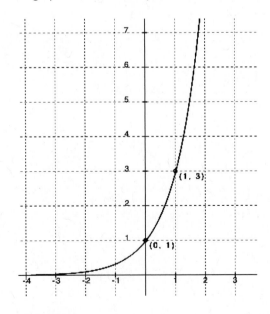

2.  Function type:

    Parent function:

    Transformations:

    Equation:

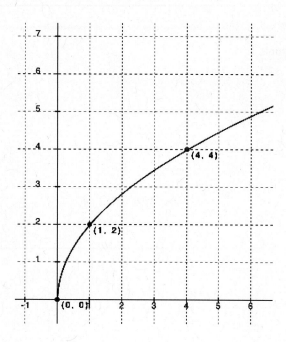

3.  Function type:

    Parent function:

    Transformations:

    Equation:

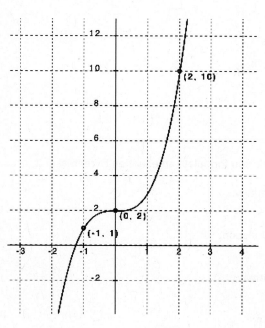

4.  Function type:

    Parent function:

    Transformations:

    Equation:

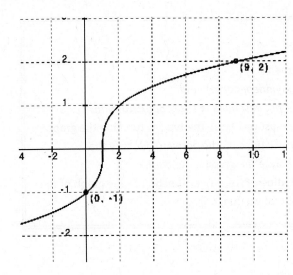

5.   Function type:

     Parent function:

     Transformations:

     Equation:

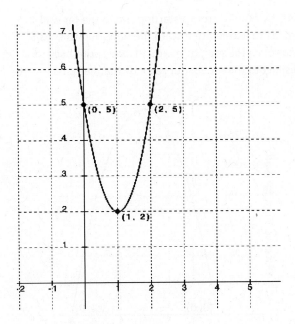

6.   Function type:

     Parent function:

     Transformations:

     Equation:

---

**Lesson Summary**

- When given a context represented graphically, you first need to:
  - *Identify the variables in the problem (dependent and independent), and*
  - *Identify the relationship between the variables that are described in the graph/situation.*
- To come up with a modeling expression from a graph, you must recognize the type of function the graph represents, observe key features of the graph (including restrictions on the domain), identify the quantities and units involved, and create an equation to analyze the graphed function.
- Identifying a parent function and thinking of the transformation of the parent function to the graph of the function can help with creating the analytical representation of the function.

---

## Problem Set

1. During tryouts for the track team, Bob is running 90-foot wind sprints by running from a starting line to the far wall of the gym and back. At time $t = 0$, he is at the starting line and ready to accelerate toward the opposite wall. As $t$ approaches 6 seconds he must slow down, stop for just an instant to touch the wall, turn around, and sprint back to the starting line. His distance, in feet, from the starting line with respect to the number of seconds that has passed for one repetition is modeled by the graph below.

   a. What are the key features of this graph?

   b. What are the units involved?

   c. What is the parent function of this graph?

   d. Were any transformations made to the parent functions to get this graph?

   e. What general analytical representation would you expect to model this context?

   f. What do you already know about the parameters of the equation?

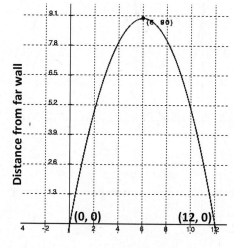

**Time (seconds)**

   g. Use the ordered pairs you know to replace the parameters in the general form of your equation with constants so that the equation will model this context. Check your answer using the graph.

---

2. Spencer and McKenna are on a long-distance bicycle ride. Spencer leaves one hour before McKenna. The graph below shows each rider's distance in miles from his or her house as a function of time since McKenna left on her bicycle to catch up with Spencer. (Note: Parts (e), (f), and (g) are challenge problems.)

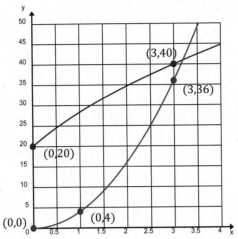

a. Which function represents Spencer's distance? Which function represents McKenna's distance? Explain your reasoning.

b. Estimate when McKenna catches up to Spencer. How far have they traveled at that point in time?

c. One rider is speeding up as time passes and the other one is slowing down. Which one is which, and how can you tell from the graphs?

d. According to the graphs, what type of function would best model each rider's distance?

e. Create a function to model each rider's distance as a function of the time since McKenna started riding her bicycle. Use the data points labeled on the graph to create a precise model for each rider's distance.

f. What is the meaning of the $x$- and $y$-intercepts of each rider in the context of this problem?

g. Estimate which rider is traveling faster 30 minutes after McKenna started riding. Show work to support your answer.

# Lesson 2:  Analyzing a Data Set

## Classwork

### Opening

When tables are used to model functions, we typically have just a few sample values of the function, and therefore have to do some detective work to figure out what the function might be.  Look at these three tables:

| $x$ | $f(x)$ |
|---|---|
| 0 | 6 |
| 1 | 12 |
| 2 | 18 |
| 3 | 24 |
| 4 | 30 |
| 5 | 36 |

| $x$ | $g(x)$ |
|---|---|
| 0 | 0 |
| 1 | 14 |
| 2 | 24 |
| 3 | 30 |
| 4 | 32 |
| 5 | 30 |

| $x$ | $h(x)$ |
|---|---|
| 0 | 1 |
| 1 | 3 |
| 2 | 9 |
| 3 | 27 |
| 4 | 81 |
| 5 | 243 |

## Example 1

Noam and Athena had an argument about whether it would take longer to get from NYC to Boston and back by car, or by train. To settle their differences, they made separate, non-stop round trips from NYC to Boston.  On the trip, at the end of each hour, both recorded the number of miles they had traveled from their starting points in NYC. The tables below show their travel times, in hours, and the distances from their starting points, in miles. The first table shows Noam's travel time/distance from the starting point, and the second represents Athena's.  Use *both* data sets to justify your answers to the questions below.

| Time in Hours | Noam's Distance |
|---------------|-----------------|
| 0 | 0 |
| 1 | 55 |
| 2 | 110 |
| 3 | 165 |
| 4 | 220 |
| 5 | 165 |
| 6 | 110 |
| 7 | 55 |
| 8 | 0 |

| Time in Hours | Athena's Distance |
|---------------|-------------------|
| 0 | 0 |
| 1 | 81 |
| 2 | 144 |
| 3 | 189 |
| 4 | 216 |
| 5 | 225 |
| 6 | 216 |
| 7 | 189 |
| 8 | 144 |
| 9 | 81 |
| 10 | 0 |

a.   Who do you think is driving, and who is riding the train?  Explain your answer in the context of the problem.

b.   According to the data, how far apart are Boston and New York City?  Explain mathematically.

c.   How long did it take each of them to make the round trip?

d.   According to their collected data, which method of travel was faster?

e.   What was the average rate of change for Athena for the interval from 3 to 4 hours?  How might you explain that in the context of the problem?

f.   Noam believes a quadratic function can be used as a model for both data sets.  Do you agree?  Use and describe the key features of the functions represented by the data sets to support your answer.

## Exercises

1. Explain why each function can or cannot be used to model the given data set:

   a. $f(x) = 3x + 5$

   | $x$ | $f(x)$ |
   |-----|--------|
   | 0   | 5      |
   | 1   | 8      |
   | 2   | 9      |
   | 3   | 8      |
   | 4   | 5      |
   | 5   | 0      |
   | 6   | -7     |

   b. $f(x) = -(x - 2)^2 + 9$

   c. $f(x) = -x^2 + 4x - 5$

   d. $f(x) = 3^x + 4$

   e. $f(x) = (x + 2)^2 - 9$

   f. $f(x) = -(x + 1)(x - 5)$

2.  Match each table below to the function and the context, and explain how you made your decision.

| A | |
|---|---|
| $x$ | $y$ |
| 1 | 9 |
| 2 | 18 |
| 3 | 27 |
| 4 | 18 |
| 5 | 9 |

| B | |
|---|---|
| $x$ | $y$ |
| 1 | 12 |
| 2 | 24 |
| 3 | 36 |
| 4 | 48 |
| 5 | 60 |

| C | |
|---|---|
| $x$ | $y$ |
| 0 | 160 |
| 1 | 174 |
| 2 | 156 |
| 3 | 106 |
| 4 | 24 |

| D | |
|---|---|
| $x$ | $y$ |
| 1 | 2 |
| 2 | 4 |
| 3 | 8 |
| 4 | 16 |
| 5 | 32 |

| E | |
|---|---|
| $x$ | $y$ |
| 2 | 8 |
| 3 | 9 |
| 4 | 8 |
| 5 | 5 |
| 6 | 0 |

Equation _____       Equation _____       Equation _____       Equation _____       Equation _____

Context _____       Context _____       Context _____       Context _____       Context _____

Equations:

$f(x) = 12x$

$h(x) = -9|x - 3| + 27$

$g(x) = -(x)(x - 6)$

$p(x) = 2^x$

$q(x) = -16x^2 + 30x + 160$

Contexts:

1.  The population of bacteria doubled every month and the total population vs. time was recorded.

2.  A ball was launched upward from the top of a building and the vertical distance of the ball from the ground vs. time was recorded.

3.  The height of a certain animal's vertical leap was recorded at regular time intervals of one second; the animal returned to ground level after six seconds.

4.  Melvin saves the same amount of money every month.  The total amount saved after each month was recorded.

5.  Chris ran at a constant rate on a straight-line path, and then returned at the same rate. His distance from his starting point was recorded at regular time intervals.

**COMMON CORE**™   | **Lesson 2:**   Analyzing a Data Set
| **Date:**   9/24/13

S.13

> **Lesson Summary**
>
> The following methods can be used to determine the appropriate model for a given data set as linear, quadratic or exponential function:
>
> - If the first difference is constant, then the data set could be modeled by a linear function.
> - If the second difference is constant, then the data set could be modeled by a quadratic function.
> - If the subsequent y-values are multiplied by a constant, then the data set could be modeled by an exponential function.

## Problem Set

1.

| $x$ | $y$ |
|---|---|
| 0 | |
| 1 | 10 |
| 2 | 0 |
| 3 | −6 |
| 4 | −8 |
| 5 | |
| 6 | |

a. Determine the function type that could be used to model the data set at the right and explain why.

b. Complete the data set using the special pattern of the function you described above.

c. If it exists, find the minimum or maximum value for the function model. If there is no minimum or maximum, explain why.

2.

| $x$ | $y$ |
|---|---|
| −1 | |
| 0 | |
| 1 | |
| 2 | 16 |
| 3 | 64 |
| 4 | 256 |
| 5 | 1024 |

a. Determine the function type that could be used to model the data set and explain why.

b. Complete the data set using the special pattern of the function you described above.

c. If it exists, find the minimum or maximum value for the function model. If there is no minimum/maximum, explain why.

3.

| $x$ | $y$ |
|---|---|
| −1 | |
| 0 | 12 |
| 1 | |
| 2 | 24 |
| 3 | |
| 4 | 36 |
| 5 | |

a. Determine the function type that could be used to model the data set and explain why.

b. Complete the data set using the special pattern of the function you described above.

c. If it exists, find the minimal or maximum value for the function model. If there is no minimum/maximum, explain why.

4.  Circle all the function types that could possibly be used to model a context if the given statement applies.

a.  When $x$-values are at regular intervals the first difference of $y$-values is not constant.

| Linear Function | Quadratic Function | Exponential Function | Absolute Value Function |

b.  The second difference of data values is not constant.

| Linear Function | Quadratic Function | Exponential Function | Absolute Value Function |

c.  When $x$-values are at regular intervals, the quotient of any two consecutive $y$-values is a constant that is not equal to 0 or 1.

| Linear Function | Quadratic Function | Exponential Function | Absolute Value Function |

d.  There maybe two different $x$-values for $y = 0$.

| Linear Function | Quadratic Function | Exponential Function | Absolute Value Function |

# Lesson 3: Analyzing a Verbal Description

## Classwork

Read the example problems below and discuss a problem solving strategy with a partner or small group.

### Example 1

Gregory plans to purchase a video game player. He has $500 in his savings account, and plans to save $20 per week from his allowance until he has enough money to buy the player. He needs to figure out how long it will take. What type of function should he use to model this problem?

### Example 2

One of the highlights in a car show event is a car driving up a ramp and 'flying' over approximately five cars placed end-to-end. The ramp is 8 feet at its highest point, and there is an upward speed of 88 feet per second before it leaves the top of the ramp.

### Example 3

Margie got $1000 from her grandmother to start her college fund. She is opening a new savings account and finds out that her bank offers a 2% annual interest rate, compounded monthly.

**Exercises**

1.  City workers recorded the number of squirrels in a park over a period of time. At the first count, there were 15 pairs of male and female squirrels (30 squirrels total). After 6 months, the scientists recorded a total of 60 squirrels, and after a year, there were 120.

    a.  What type of function can best model the population of squirrels recorded over a period of time, assuming the same growth rate and that no squirrel dies?

    b.  Write a function that represents the population of squirrels recorded over $x$ number of years. Explain how you determined your function.

2.  A rectangular photograph measuring 8 inches by 10 inches is surrounded by a frame with a uniform width, $x$.

    a.  What type of function can best represent the area of the picture and the frame in terms of $x$ (the unknown frame's width)? Explain mathematically how you know.

    b.  Write an equation in standard form representing the area of the picture and the frame. Explain how you arrive at your equation.

3. A ball is tossed up in the air at an initial rate of 50 feet per second from 5 feet off the ground.

    a.   What type of function models the height ($h$, in feet) of the ball after $t$ seconds?

    b.   Explain what is happening to the height of the ball as it travels over a period of time (in $t$ seconds)?

    c.   What function models the height, $h$ (in feet), of the ball over a period of time (in $t$ seconds)?

4. A population of insects is known to triple in size every month. At the beginning of a scientific research project, there were 200 insects.

    a.   What type of function models the population of the insects after $t$ years?

    b.   Write a function that models the population growth of the insects after $t$ years?

---

**Lesson Summary**

The following methods can be used to recognize a function type from a word problem:

1.  If a problem requires repeated adding or subtracting a constant value, then it is represented by a linear function.

2.  If a problem involves free-falling motion of object or an area, then it is represented by a quadratic function.

3.  If a problem is about population growth or compound interest, then it is represented by an exponential function.

---

Problem Set

1.  The costs to purchase school spirit posters are as follows:  two posters for $5, four posters for $9, six posters for $13, eight posters for $17, and so on.

    a.  What type of function would best represent the cost of the total number of posters purchased?

    b.  What function represents the cost of the total number of posters purchased?  How did you know?  Justify your reasoning.

    c.  If you have $40 to spend, write an inequality to find the maximum number of posters you could buy.

2.  NYC Sports Gym had 425 members in 2011.  Based on statistics, the total number of memberships increases by 2% annually.

    a.  What type of function models the total number of memberships in this situation?

    b.  If the trend continues, what function represents the total number of memberships in $n$ years?  How did you know?  Justify your reasoning.

3.  Derek hits a baseball thrown by the pitcher with an initial upward speed of 60 feet per second from a height of 3 feet.

    a.  What type of function models the height of the baseball versus time since it was hit?

    b.  What is the function that models the height, $h$ (in feet), the baseball travels over a period of time in $t$ seconds?  How did you know?  Justify your reasoning.

---

| Lesson 3: | Analyzing a Verbal Description |
|-----------|-------------------------------|
| Date:     | 10/4/13                       |

S.19

# Lesson 4:  Modeling a Context from a Graph

**Opening Exercise**

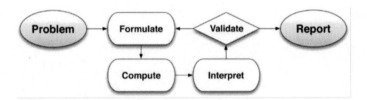

**Example 1**

Read the problem below.  Your teacher will walk you through the process of using the steps in the modeling cycle to guide in your solution:

The relationship between the length of one of the legs, in feet, of an animal and its walking speed, in feet per second, can be modeled by the graph below.  [Note:  This function applies to *walking* not *running* speed.  Obviously, a cheetah has shorter legs than a giraffe, but can run much faster.  However, in a walking race, the giraffe has the advantage.]

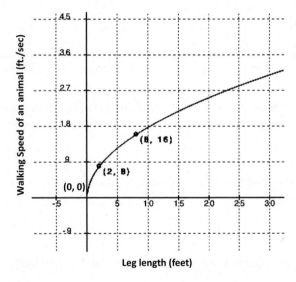

Leg length (feet)

A T-Rex's leg length was 20 ft.  What was the T-Rex's speed in ft./sec.?

## Exercises

Now practice using the modeling cycle with these problems:

1.  Eduardo has a summer job that pays him a certain rate for the first 40 hours per week and time and a half for any overtime. The graph below is a representation of how much money he earns as a function of the hours he works in one week.

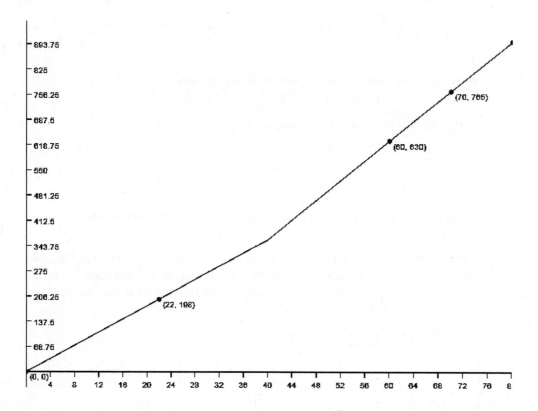

Eduardo's employers want to make him a salaried employee, which means he does not get overtime. If they want to pay him 480 dollars a week but have him commit to 50 hours a week, should he agree to the salary change? Justify your answer mathematically.

a.   *FORMULATE*  (recall this step from Lesson 1).

   i.   What type of function can be represented by a graph like this (e.g., quadratic, linear, exponential, piecewise, square root, or cube root)?

   ii.   How would you describe the end-behavior of the graph in the context of this problem?

   iii.   How does this affect the equation of our function?

b.  COMPUTE

  i.   What strategy do you plan to use to come up with the model for this context?

  ii.  Find the function of this graph.  Show all your work.

c.  INTERPRET

  i.   How much does Eduardo make an hour?

  ii.  By looking only at the graphs, which interval has a greater average rate of change: $x < 20$, or $x > 45$?
       Justify your answer by making connections to the graph and its verbal description.

  iii. Eduardo's employers want to make Eduardo a salaried employee, which means he does not get overtime.
       If they want to pay him 480 dollars a week but have him commit to 50 hours a week, should he agree to
       the salary change?  Justify your answer mathematically.

d.  VALIDATE

    i.  How can you check to make sure your function models the graph accurately?

2.  The cross-section view of a deep river gorge is modeled by the graph shown below where both height and distance are measured in miles.  How long is a bridge that spans the gorge from the point labeled (1,0) to the other side? How high above the bottom of the gorge is the bridge?

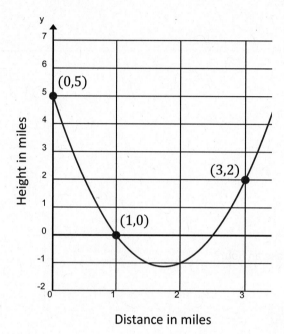

Distance in miles

a.  FORMULATE

    i.  What type of function can be represented by a graph like this?  (Linear, quadratic, exponential, piecewise, square root, or cube root)

    ii.  What are the quantities in this problem?

    iii.  How would you describe the end-behavior of the graph?

iv. What is a general form for this function type?


v. How does knowing the function type and end-behavior affect the equation of the function for this graph?


vi. What is the equation we would use to model this graph?


b. COMPUTE

i. What are the key features of the graph that can be used to determine the equation?


ii. Which key features of the function must be determined?


iii. Calculate the missing key features and check for accuracy with your graph.

c.  INTERPRET

    i.    What domain makes sense for this context?  Explain.

    ii.    How wide is the bridge with one side located at $(1,0)$?

    iii.    How high is the bridge above the bottom of the gorge?

    iv.    Suppose the gorge is exactly 3.5 feet wide from its two highest points.  Find the average rate of change for the interval from $x = 0$ to $x = 3.5$, $[0, 3.5]$.  Explain this phenomenon.  Are there other intervals that will behave similarly?

d.  VALIDATE

    i.    How can you check to make sure that your function models the graph accurately?

Now compare four representations that may be involved in the modeling process.  How is each useful for each phase of the modeling cycle?  Explain the advantages and disadvantages of each.

**Lesson Summary**

When modeling from a graph use the full modeling cycle:

- FORMULATE – identify the variables involved, classify the type of graph presented, point out the visible key features, and create a different representation of the relationship if needed.
- COMPUTE – decontextualize the graph from the application and analyze it.  You might have to find symbolic or tabular representation of the graph to further analyze it.
- INTERPRET – contextualize the features of the function and your results and make sense of them in the context provided.
- VALIDATE – check your results with the context.  Do your answers make sense?  Are the calculations accurate?  Are there possibilities for error?
- REPORT – clearly write your results.

**Problem Set**

1.  During tryouts for the track team, Bob is running 90-foot wind sprints by running from a starting line to the far wall of the gym and back.  At time, $t = 0$, he is at the starting line and ready to accelerate toward the opposite wall.  As $t$ approaches 6 seconds, he must slow down, stop for just an instant to touch the wall, then turn around, and sprint back to the starting line.  His distance, in feet, from the starting line with respect to the number of seconds that has passed for one repetition, is modeled by the graph below.

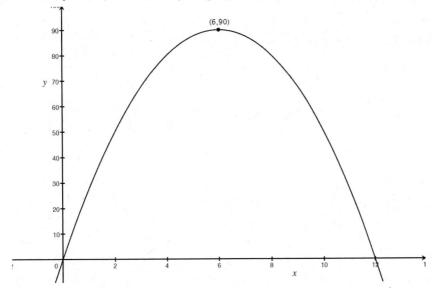

(Note:  You may refer to Lesson 1, Problem Set #1 to help answer this question.)

How far was Bob from the starting line at 2 seconds?  6.5 seconds?  (Distances, in meters, should be represented to the nearest tenth.)

2. Kyle and Abed each threw a baseball across a field. The height of the balls is described by functions $A(t)$ and $K(t)$, where $t$ is the number of seconds the baseball is in the air. $K(t)$ (equation below left) models the height of Kyle's baseball and $A(t)$ models the height of Abed's baseball (graph below):

$$K(t) = -16t^2 + 66t + 6$$

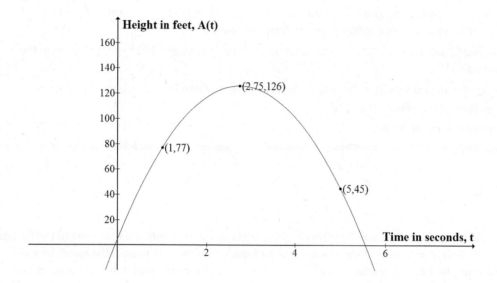

a. Which ball was in the air for a longer period of time?

b. Whose ball goes higher?

c. How high was Abed's ball when he threw it?

# Lesson 5: Modeling from a Sequence

## Classwork

### Opening Exercise

A soccer coach is getting her students ready for the season by introducing them to High Intensity Interval Training (HIIT). She presents the table below with a list of exercises for an HIIT training circuit and the length of time that must be spent on each exercise before the athlete gets a short time to rest. The rest times increase as the students complete more exercises in the circuit. Study the chart and answer the questions below. How long would the 10th exercise be? If a player had 30 minutes of actual gym time during a period, how many exercises could she get done? Explain your answers.

| Exercise # | Length of Exercise Time | Length of Rest Time |
|---|---|---|
| Exercise 1 | 0.5 minutes | 0.25 minutes |
| Exercise 2 | 0.75 minutes | 0.5 minutes |
| Exercise 3 | 1 minute | 1 minutes |
| Exercise 4 | 1.25 minutes | 2 minutes |
| Exercise 5 | 1.5 minutes | 4 minutes |

### Example 1

Determine whether the sequence below is arithmetic or geometric and to find the function that will produce any given term in the sequence:

$$16, 24, 36, 54, 81, \ldots$$

Is this sequence arithmetic?

Is the sequence geometric?

What is the analytical representation of the sequence?

**Exercises**

Look at the sequence and determine the analytical representation of the sequence. Show your work and reasoning.

1.  A decorating consultant charges $50 for the first hour and $2 for each additional whole hour. How much would 1000 hours of consultation cost?

| $n$ | 1 | 2 | 3 | 4 | 5 | ... | $n$ |
|---|---|---|---|---|---|---|---|
| $f(n)$ | 50 | 52 | 54 | 56 | 58 | | ? |

2.  The sequence below represents the area of a square whose side length is the diagonal of a square with integer side length n. What would be the area for the 100$^{th}$ square? [Hint: You can use the square below to find the function model, but you can also just use the terms of the sequence.]

| $n$ | 1 | 2 | 3 | 4 | 5 | ... | $n$ |
|---|---|---|---|---|---|---|---|
| $f(n)$ | 2 | 8 | 18 | 32 | 50 | | ? |

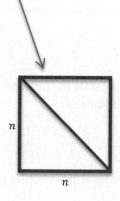

3.  What would be the 10<sup>th</sup> term in the sequence?

| $n$ | 1 | 2 | 3 | 4 | ... | $n$ |
|------|---|---|---|---|-----|-----|
| $f(n)$ | 3 | 6 | 12 | 24 | | ? |

---

**Lesson Summary**

- A sequence is a list of numbers or objects in a special order.

- An arithmetic sequence goes from one term to the next by adding (or subtracting) the same value.

- A geometric sequence goes from one term to the next by multiplying (or dividing) by the same value.

- Looking at the difference of differences can be a quick way to determine if a sequence can be represented as a quadratic expression.

---

## Problem Set

Solve the following problems by finding the function/formula that represents the $n^{th}$ term of the sequence.

1. After a knee injury, a jogger is told he can jog 10 minutes every day, and that he can increase his jogging time by 2 minutes every two weeks. How long will it take for him to be able to jog one hour a day?

| Week # | Daily Jog Time |
|--------|----------------|
| 1 | 10 |
| 2 | 10 |
| 3 | 12 |
| 4 | 12 |
| 5 | 14 |
| 6 | 14 |

2. A ball is dropped from a height of 10 feet. The ball then bounces to 80% of its previous height with each subsequent bounce.

    a. Explain how this situation can be modeled with a sequence.

    b. How high (*to the nearest tenth of a foot*) does the ball bounce on the fifth bounce?

3. Consider the following sequence:

$$8, 17, 32, 53, 80, 113, \ldots$$

    a. What pattern do you see, and what does that pattern mean for the analytical representation of the function?

    b. What is the symbolic representation of the sequence?

4. Arnold wants to be able to complete 100 military-style pull-ups. His trainer puts him on a workout regimen designed to improve his pull-up strength. The following chart shows how many pull-ups Arnold can complete after each month of training. How many months will it take Arnold to achieve his goal if this pattern continues?

| Month | Pull-Up Count |
|-------|---------------|
| 1 | 2 |
| 2 | 5 |
| 3 | 10 |
| 4 | 17 |
| 5 | 26 |
| 6 | 37 |
| ... | |
| | |

---

# Lesson 6: Modeling a Context from Data

## Classwork

### Opening Exercise

1. Identify the type of function the each table represents (e.g., quadratic, linear, exponential, square root, etc.).

2. Explain how you were able to identify the function.

3. Find the symbolic representation of the function.

| A | | | B | | | C | |
|---|---|---|---|---|---|---|---|
| $x$ | $y$ | | $x$ | $y$ | | $x$ | $y$ |
| 1 | 5 | | 1 | 6 | | 1 | 3 |
| 2 | 7 | | 2 | 9 | | 2 | 12 |
| 3 | 9 | | 3 | 13.5 | | 3 | 27 |
| 4 | 11 | | 4 | 20.25 | | 4 | 48 |
| 5 | 13 | | 5 | 30.375 | | 5 | 75 |

4. Plot the graphs of your data.

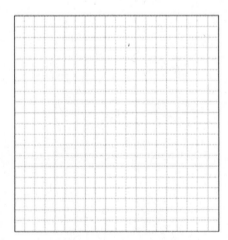
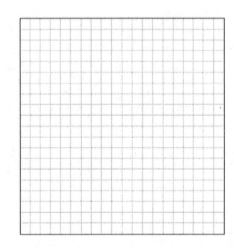
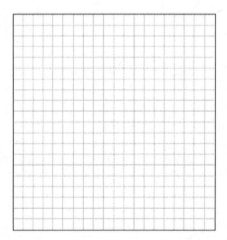

### Example 1

Enrique is a biologist who has been monitoring the population of a rare fish in Lake Placid. He has tracked the population for 5 years, and has come up with the following estimates:

| Year Tracked | Year since 2002 | Estimated Fish Population |
|:---:|:---:|:---:|
| 2002 | 0 | 1000 |
| 2003 | 1 | 899 |
| 2004 | 2 | 796 |
| 2005 | 3 | 691 |
| 2006 | 4 | 584 |

Create a graph and a function to model this situation and use it to predict (assuming the trend continues) when the fish population will be gone from the Lake Placid ecosystem. Verify your results, and explain the limitations of each model.

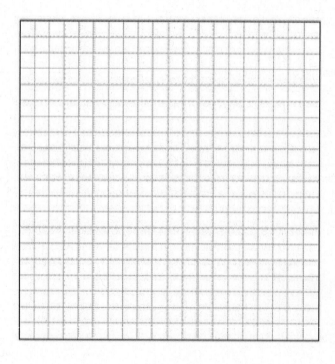

## Exercises

1.  Bella is a BMX bike racer and wants to identify the relationship between her bike's weight and the height of jumps (a category she gets judged on when racing).  On a practice course, she tests out 7 bike models with different weights and comes up with the following data.

| Weight (lbs.) | Height (ft.) |
| --- | --- |
| 20 | 8.9 |
| 21 | 8.82 |
| 22 | 8.74 |
| 23 | 8.66 |
| 24 | 8.58 |
| 25 | 8.5 |
| 26 | 8.42 |
| 27 | 8.34 |

a.  Bella is sponsored by Twilight Bikes and must ride a 32-lb bike.  What can she expect her jump height to be?

b.  Bella asks the bike engineers at Twilight to make the lightest bike possible.  They tell her the lightest functional bike they could make is 10 lbs.  Based on this data, what is the highest she should expect to jump if she only uses Twilight bikes?

c.  What is the maximum weight of a bike if Bella's jumps have to be at least 2 feet high during a race?

2.  The concentration of medicine in a patient's blood as time passes is recorded in the table below.

| Time (hours) | Concentration of Medicine (ml) |
|:---:|:---:|
| 0 | 0 |
| 0.5 | 55.5 |
| 1 | 83 |
| 1.5 | 82.5 |
| 2 | 54 |

a.  The patient cannot be active while the medicine is in his blood.  How long, to the nearest minute, must the patient remain inactive?  What are the limitations of your model(s)?

b.  What is the highest concentration of medicine in the patient's blood?

3.  A student is conducting an experiment and, as time passes, the number of cells in the experiment decreases. How many cells will there be after 16 minutes?

| Time (minutes) | Cells |
|:---:|:---:|
| 0 | 5,000,000 |
| 1 | 2,750,000 |
| 2 | 1,512,500 |
| 3 | 831,875 |
| 4 | 457,531 |
| 5 | 251,642 |
| 6 | 138,403 |

---

**Lesson Summary**

When given a data set, strategies that could be used to determine the type of function that describes the relationship between the data are:

- Determine the variables involved and plot the points.
- After making sure the $x$-values are given at regular intervals, look for common differences between the data points – first and second.
- Determine the type of sequence the data models first, then use the general form of the function equation to find the parameters for the symbolic representation of the function.

---

| Lesson 6: | Modeling a Context from Data |
|---|---|
| Date: | 9/25/13 |

S.36

# Lesson 7: Modeling a Context from Data

## Classwork

### Opening Exercise

What is this data table telling us?

| Age (Years) | NYC Marathon Running Time (Minutes) |
|:-----------:|:-----------------------------------:|
| 15 | 300 |
| 25 | 190 |
| 35 | 180 |
| 45 | 200 |
| 55 | 225 |
| 65 | 280 |

### Example 1

Remember that in Module 2, we used a graphing display calculator (GDC) to find a linear regression model. If a linear model is not appropriate for a collection of data, it may be possible that a quadratic or exponential will be a better fit. Your graphing calculator is capable of determining various types of regressions. Use a graphing display calculator (GDC) to determine if a data set has a better fit with a quadratic or exponential function. You may need to review entering the data into the stats application of your GDC.

When you are ready to begin, return to the data presented in the Opening Exercise. Use your graphing calculator to determine the function that best fits the data. Then, answer some questions your teacher will ask about the data.

**Exercises**

1.  Use the following data table to construct a regression model, then answer the questions:

| Chicken Breast Frying Time (Minutes) | Moisture Content (%) |
|---|---|
| 5 | 16.3 |
| 10 | 9.7 |
| 15 | 8.1 |
| 20 | 4.2 |
| 25 | 3.4 |
| 30 | 2.9 |
| 45 | 1.9 |
| 60 | 1.3 |

Data Source: *Journal of Food Processing and Preservation*, 1995.

a.  What function type appears to be the best fit for this data?  Explain how you know.

b.  A student chooses a quadratic regression to model this data.  Is he right or wrong?  Why or why not?

c.  Will the moisture content for this product ever reach 0%?  Why or why not?

d.  Based on this model, what would you expect the moisture content to be of a chicken breast fried for 50 minutes?

2. Use the following data table to construct a regression model, then answer the questions based on your model.

**Prevalence of No Leisure-Time Activities, 1988 - 2008**

| Year | Years since 1988 | % of prevalence |
|------|------------------|-----------------|
| 1988 | 0 | 30.5 |
| 1989 | 1 | 31.5 |
| 1990 | 2 | 30.9 |
| 1991 | 3 | 30.6 |
| 1992 | 4 | 29.3 |
| 1994 | 6 | 30.2 |
| 1996 | 8 | 28.4 |
| 1998 | 10 | 28.4 |
| 2000 | 12 | 27.8 |
| 2001 | 13 | 26.2 |
| 2002 | 14 | 25.1 |
| 2003 | 15 | 24.2 |
| 2004 | 16 | 23.7 |
| 2005 | 17 | 25.1 |
| 2006 | 18 | 23.9 |
| 2007 | 19 | 23.9 |
| 2008 | 20 | 25.1 |

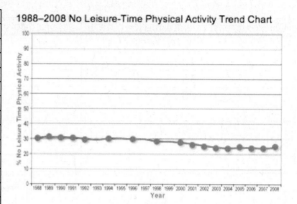

1988–2008 No Leisure-Time Physical Activity Trend Chart

a. What trends do you see in this collection of data?

b. How do you interpret this trend?

c. If the trend continues, what would we expect the percentage of people in the U.S. who report no leisure-time physical activity to be in 2020?

---

**Lesson Summary**

- Using data plots and other visual displays of data the function type that appears to be the best fit for the data can be determined. Using the correlation coefficient the measure of the strength and the direction of a linear relationship can be determined.

- A graphing calculator can be used if the data sets are imperfect. To find a regression equation, the same steps will be performed as for a linear regression.

---

**Problem Set**

1.  Use the following data tables to write a regression model, then answer the questions:

Prescription Drug Sales in the United States Since 1995

| Years Since 1995 | Prescription Drug Sales (billions of $USD) |
|---|---|
| 0 | 68.6 |
| 2 | 81.9 |
| 3 | 103.0 |
| 4 | 121.7 |
| 5 | 140.7 |

a.  What is the best model for this data?

b.  Based on your model, what would you expect prescription drug sales to be in 2002? 2005?

c.  For this model, would it make sense to input negative values for $t$ into your regression? Why or why not?

2.  Use the data below to answer the questions that follow:

Per Capita Ready-to-Eat Cereal Consumption in the United States per Year Since 1980

| Years Since 1980 | Cereal Consumption (lbs.) | Years Since 1980 | Cereal Consumption (lbs.) |
|---|---|---|---|
| 0 | 12 | 10 | 15.4 |
| 1 | 12 | 11 | 16.1 |
| 2 | 11.9 | 12 | 16.6 |
| 3 | 12.2 | 13 | 17.3 |
| 4 | 12.5 | 14 | 17.4 |
| 5 | 12.8 | 15 | 17.1 |
| 6 | 13.1 | 16 | 16.6 |
| 7 | 13.3 | 17 | 16.3 |
| 8 | 14.2 | 18 | 15.6 |
| 9 | 14.9 | 19 | 15.5 |

a.  What is the best model for this data?

b.  Based on your model, what would you expect per capita cereal consumption to be in 2002? 2005?

c.  For this model, will it make sense to input $t$-values that return negative $f(t)$-values into your regression? Why or why not?

---

Lesson 7:   Modeling a Context from Data
Date:       10/4/13

S.40

# Lesson 8: Modeling a Context from a Verbal Description

## Classwork

### Example 1

Christine has $500 to deposit in a savings account and she is trying to decide between two banks. Bank A offers 10% annual interest compounded quarterly. Rather than compounding interest for smaller accounts, Bank B offers to add $15 quarterly to any account with a balance of less than $1000 for every quarter, as long as there are no withdrawals. Christine has decided that she will neither withdraw, nor make a deposit for a number of years.

Develop a model that will help Christine decide which bank to use.

### Example 2

Alex designed a new snowboard. He wants to market it and make a profit. The total initial cost for manufacturing set-up, advertising, etc. is $500,000 and the materials to make the snowboards cost $100 per board.

The demand function for selling a similar snowboard is: $D(p) = 50{,}000 - 100p$, where $p$ = selling price of each snowboard.

a. Write an expression for each of the following. Let $p$ represent the selling price:

Demand Function (number of units that will sell)

Revenue (number of units that will sell, price per unit, $p$)

Total Cost (cost for producing the snowboards)

b.   Write an expression to represent the profit.

c.   What is the selling price of the snowboard that will give the maximum profit?

d.   What is the maximum profit Alex can make?

## Exercises

Alvin just turned 16 years old. His grandmother told him that she will give him $10,000 to buy any car he wants whenever he is ready.  Alvin wants to be able to buy his dream car by his 21st birthday and he wants a 2009 Avatar Z, which he could purchase today for $25,000.  The car depreciates (reduces in value) at a rate is 15% per year.  He wants to figure out how long it would take for his $10,000 to be enough to buy the car, without investing it.

1.   Write the function that models the depreciated value of the car after $n$ number of years?

| After $n$ years | Value of the Car |
|---|---|
| 1 | |
| 2 | |
| 3 | |
| 4 | |
| 5 | |
| 6 | |

a.   Will he be able to afford to buy the car when he turns 21?  Explain why or why not.

b.   Given the same rate of depreciation, after how many years will the value of the car be less than $5000?

c.  If the same rate of depreciation were to continue indefinitely, after how many years would the value of the car be approximately $1?

2.  Sophia plans to invest $1000 in each of three banks.

Bank A offers an annual interest rate of 12%, compounded annually.

Bank B offers an annual interest rate of 12%, compounded quarterly.

Bank C offers an annual interest rate of 12%, compounded monthly.

a.  Write the function that describes the growth of investment for each bank in $n$ years?

b.  How many years will it take to double her initial investment for each bank? (Round to the nearest whole dollar.)

| Year | Bank A | Bank B | Bank C |
|---|---|---|---|
| Year 1 | | | |
| Year 2 | | | |
| Year 3 | | | |
| Year 4 | | | |
| Year 5 | | | |
| Year 6 | | | |
| Year 7 | | | |

c.  Sophia went to Bank D.  The bank offers a "double your money program" for an initial investment of $1000 in five years, compounded annually.  What is the annual interest rate for Bank D?

Lesson 8:       Modeling a Context from a Verbal Description
Date:           10/4/13

---

**Lesson Summary**

- We can use the full modeling cycle is used to solve real world problems in the context of business and commerce (e.g., compound interest, revenue, profit, and cost) and population growth and decay (e.g., population growth, depreciation value, and half-life) to demonstrate linear, exponential and quadratic functions described verbally through using graphs, tables, or algebraic expressions to make appropriate interpretation and decision.

- Sometimes a graph or table is the best model for problems that involve complicated function equations.

---

**Problem Set**

1. Maria invested $10,000 in the stock market. Unfortunately, the value of her investment has been dropping at an average rate of 3% each year.

   a. Write the function that best models the situation.

   b. If the trend continues, how much will her investment be worth in 5 years?
      (For $n = 5$)

   c. Given the situation, what should she do with her investment?

2. The half-life of the radioactive material in *Z-Med*, a medication used for certain types of therapy, is 2 days. A patient receives a 16-mCi dose (millicuries, a measure of radiation) in his treatment. [Half-life means that the radioactive material decays to the point where only half is left.]

   a. Make a table to show the level of *Z-Med* in the patient's body after $n$ days.

      | Number of days | Level of *Z-Med* in patient |
      |:---:|:---:|
      | 0 | |
      | 2 | |
      | 4 | |
      | 6 | |
      | 8 | |
      | 10 | |

   b. Write an equation for $f(n)$ to model the half-life of *Z-Med* for $n$ days. [Be careful here. Make sure that the formula works for both odd and even numbers of days.]

   c. How much radioactive material from *Z-Med* is left in the patient's body after 20 days of receiving the medicine?

---

3. Suppose a male and a female of a certain species of animal were taken to a deserted island. The population of this species quadruples (multiplies by 4) every year. Assume that the animals have an abundant food supply and no predators on the island.

   a. What is an equation that can be used to model the number of offspring the animals will produce?

   b. What will the population of the species be after 5 years?

| After $n$ years | Population |
|---|---|
| 0 | |
| 1 | |
| 2 | |
| 3 | |
| 4 | |
| 5 | |

   c. Write an equation to find how many years it will take for the population of the animals to exceed 1 million. Find the number of years, either by using the equation or a table.

4. The revenue of a company for a given month is represented as $R(x) = 1,500x - x^2$, and its costs as $C(x) = 1,500 + 1,000x$. What is the selling price, $x$, of their product that would yield the maximum profit? Show or explain your answer.

| After $n$ years | Population |
|---|---|
| 0 | |
| 1 | |
| 2 | |
| 3 | |
| 4 | |
| 5 | |
| 6 | |
| 7 | |
| 8 | |
| 9 | |
| 10 | |

# Lesson 9:  Modeling a Context from a Verbal Description

**Opening Exercise**

What does it mean to "attend to precision" when modeling in mathematics?

## Example 1

Marymount Township secured the construction of a power plant in 1990.  Once the power plant was built, the population of Marymount increased by about 20% each year for the first ten years, and then increased by 5% each year after that.

    a.   If the population was 150,000 people in 2010, what was the population in 2000?

<u>Precision</u>

    b.   How should you round your answer?  Explain.

    c.   What was the population in 1990?

**Example 2**

If the trend continued, what would the population be in 2009?

**Exercises**

1.  A tortoise and a hare are having a race.  The tortoise moves at 4 miles per hour.  The hare travels at 10 miles per hour.  Halfway through the race, the hare decides to take a 5-hour nap and then gets up and continues at 10 miles per hour.

    a.  If the race is 40 miles long, who won the race?  Support your answer with mathematical evidence.

    b.  How long (in miles) would the race have to be for there to be a tie between the two creatures, if the same situation (as described in Exercise 1) happened?

2. The graph on the right represents the value $V$ of a popular stock. Its initial value was $12/share on day 0.

Note: The calculator uses $X$ to represent $t$, and $Y$ to represent $V$.

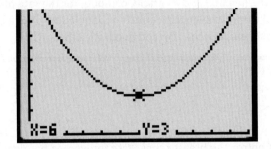

a. How many days after its initial value at time $t = 0$ did the stock price return to $12 per share?

b. Write a quadratic equation representing the value of this stock over time.

c. Use this quadratic equation to predict the stock's value after 15 days.

Lesson Summary

The full modeling cycle is used to interpret the function and its graph, compute for the rate of change over an interval and attend to precision to solve real world problems in context of population growth and decay and other problems in geometric sequence or forms of linear, exponential and quadratic functions.

Problem Set

1. According to the Center for Disease and Control, the breast cancer rate for women has decreased at 0.9% per year between 2000–2009.

   a. If 192,370 women were diagnosed with invasive breast cancer in 2009, how many were diagnosed in 2005? For this problem, assume that the there is no change in population from 2005 and 2009.

   b. According to the American Cancer Society, in 2005 there were 211,240 people diagnosed with breast cancer. In a written response, communicate how precise and accurate your solution in part (a) is, and explain why.

2. The functions $f(x)$ and $g(x)$ represent the population of two different kinds of bacteria, where $x$ is the time (in hours) and $f(x)$ and $g(x)$ are the number of bacteria (in thousands). $f(x) = 2x^2 + 7$ and $g(x) = 2^x$.

   a. Between the third and sixth hour, which bacteria had a faster rate of growth?

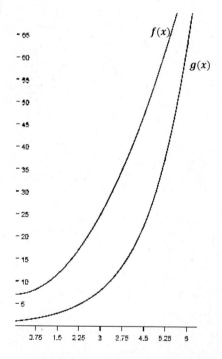

   b. Will the population of $g(x)$ ever exceed the population of $f(x)$? If so at what hour?

# Copy Ready Materials

Name _____    Date_____

# Lesson 1:  Analyzing a Graph

Exit Ticket

Read the problem description and answer the questions below.  Use a separate piece of paper if needed.

A library posted a graph in its display case to illustrate the relationship between the fee for any given late day for a borrowed book and the total number of days the book is overdue.  The graph, shown below, includes a few data points for reference.  Rikki has forgotten this policy and wants to know what her fine would be for a given number of late days.

*[Note:  The ordered pairs may be difficult to read. They are:  $(1, 0.1)$ $(10, 1)$ and $(11, 1.5)$ $(14, 3)$.]*

1.  What type of function is this?

2.  What is the general form of the parent function(s) of this graph?

3.  What equations would you expect to use to model this context?

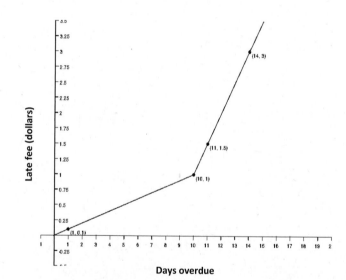

4.  Describe verbally what this graph is telling you about the library fees.

5. Compare the advantages and disadvantages of the graph versus the equation as a model for this relationship. What would be the advantage of using a verbal description in this context? How might you use a table of values?

6. What suggestions would you make to the library for how they could better share this information with their customers? Comment on the accuracy and helpfulness of this graph.

Name _____     Date_____

# Lesson 2:  Analyzing a Data Set

Analyze these data sets, recognizing the unique pattern and key feature(s) for each relationship.  Then use your findings to fill in the missing data, match to the correct function from the list on the right, and describe the key feature(s) that helped you choose the function.

**Table A**

| $x$ | $y$ |
|---|---|
| 0 | 6 |
| 1 | 10 |
| 2 | 14 |
| 3 | ◯ |
| 4 | 22 |
| 5 | ◯ |

**Table B**

| $x$ | $y$ |
|---|---|
| 0 | 6 |
| 1 | 15 |
| 2 | 18 |
| 3 | 15 |
| 4 | ◯ |
| 5 | ◯ |

**Table C**

| $x$ | $y$ |
|---|---|
| $-1$ | $\dfrac{1}{6}$ |
| 0 | 1 |
| 1 | ◯ |
| 2 | 36 |
| 3 | ◯ |
| 4 | 1296 |

**Table D**

| $x$ | $y$ |
|---|---|
| $-1$ | ◯ |
| 0 | 6 |
| 1 | 8 |
| 2 | 6 |
| 3 | 0 |
| 4 | ◯ |
| 5 | $-24$ |

*Equations:*

$f(x) = 6^x$

$h(x) = -3(x - 2)^2 + 18$

$g(x) = -2(x + 1)(x - 3)$

$r(x) = 4x + 6$

Table A: _____ Key Feature(s): _____

Table B: _____ Key Feature(s): _____

Table C: _____ Key Feature(s): _____

Table D: _____ Key Feature(s): _____

Name _____     Date_____

# Lesson 3:  Analyzing a Verbal Description

Exit Ticket

Create a model to compare these two texting plans:

i.   Plan A costs $15 a month, including 200 free texts.  After 200, they cost $0.15 each.

ii.  Plan B costs $20 a month, including 250 free texts.  After 250, they cost $0.10 each.

Name _____     Date_____

# Lesson 4:  Modeling a Context from a Graph

Exit Ticket

1.   Why might we want to represent a graph of a function in analytical form?

2.   Why might we want to represent a graph as a table of values?

Name _____     Date_____

# Lesson 5:  Modeling From a Sequence

Exit Ticket

1.  A culture of bacteria doubles every 2 hours.

    a.  Explain how this situation can be modeled with a sequence.

    b.  If there are 500 bacteria at the beginning, how many bacteria will there be after 24 hours?

Name _____     Date_____

# Lesson 6:  Modeling a Context From Data

Exit Ticket

1.  Lewis' dad put 1,000 dollars in a money market fund with a fixed interest rate when he was 16.  Lewis can't touch the money until he is 26, but he gets updates on the balance of his account.

| Years After Lewis Turns 16 | Account Balance in Dollars |
|:---:|:---:|
| 0 | 1000 |
| 1 | 1100 |
| 2 | 1210 |
| 3 | 1331 |
| 4 | 1464 |

a.   Develop a model for this situation.

b.   Use your model to determine how much Lewis will have when he turns 26 years old.

c.   Comment on the limitations/validity of your model.

Name _____     Date_____

# Lesson 7:  Modeling a Context From Data

Exit Ticket

1.  Use the following data table to construct a regression model, then answer the questions:

| Shoe Length (inches) | Height (inches) |
|---|---|
| 11.4 | 68 |
| 11.6 | 67 |
| 11.8 | 65 |
| 11.8 | 71 |
| 12.2 | 69 |
| 12.2 | 69 |
| 12.2 | 71 |
| 12.6 | 72 |
| 12.6 | 74 |
| 12.8 | 70 |

a.   What is the best regression model for the data?

b.   Based on your regression model, what height would you expect a person with a shoe length of 13.4 inches to be?

c.   Interpret the value of your correlation coefficient in the context of the problem.

Name _____   Date_____

# Lesson 8:  Modeling a Context From a Verbal Description

**Exit Ticket**

Answer the following question.  Look back at this (or other) lessons if you need help with the business formulas.

Jerry and Carlos each have $1000 and are trying to increase their savings.  Jerry will keep his money at home and add $50 per month from his part time job.  Carlos will put his money in a bank account that earns a 4% yearly interest rate, compounded monthly.  Who has a better plan for increasing his savings?

Name _____     Date_____

# Lesson 9:  Modeling a Context From a Verbal Description

Exit Ticket

The distance a car travels before coming to a stop once a driver hits the brakes is related to the speed of the car when the brakes were applied.  The graph of $f$ (shown below) is a model of the stopping distance (in feet) of a car traveling at different speeds (in miles per hour).

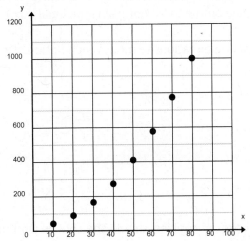

1.  One data point on the graph of $f$ appears to be (80,1000).  What do you think this point represents in the context of this problem.  Explain your reasoning.


2.  Estimate the stopping distance of the car if the driver is traveling at 65 mph when she hits the brakes.  Explain how you got your answer.


3.  Estimate the average rate of change of $f$ between $x = 50$ and $x = 60$.  What is the meaning of the rate of change in the context of this problem?


4.  What information would help you make a better prediction about stopping distance and average rate of change for this situation?

Name _____     Date _____

1. In their entrepreneurship class, students are given two options for ways to earn a commission selling cookies. For both options, students will be paid according to the number of boxes they are able to sell, with commissions being paid only after all sales have ended. Students must commit to one commission option before they begin selling.

   Option 1: The commission for each box of cookies sold is 2 dollars.
   Option 2: The commission will be based on the total number of boxes of cookies sold as follows: 2 cents is the total commission if one box is sold, 4 cents is the commission if two boxes are sold, 8 cents if three boxes are sold, and so on, doubling the amount for each additional box sold. (This option is based upon the total number of boxes sold and is paid on the total, not each individual box.)

   a. Define the variables and write function equations to model each option. Describe the domain for each function.

   b. If Barbara thinks she can sell five boxes of cookies, should she choose Option 1 or 2?

   c. Which option should she choose if she thinks she can sell ten boxes? Explain.

d.  How many boxes of cookies would a student have to sell before Option 2 pays more than Option 1? Show your work and verify your answer graphically.

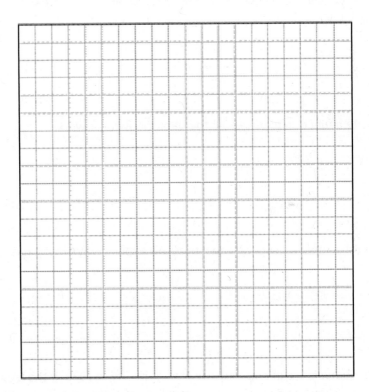

2.  The table shows the average sale price $p$ of a house in New York City, for various years $t$ since 1960.

| Years since 1960, $t$ | 0 | 1 | 2 | 3 | 4 | 5 | 6 |
|---|---|---|---|---|---|---|---|
| Average sale price (in thousands of dollars), $p$ | 45 | 36 | 29 | 24 | 21 | 20 | 21 |

a.  What type of function most appropriately represents this set of data? Explain your reasoning.

b.  In what year is the price at the lowest? Explain how you know.

c.  Write a function to represent the data. Show your work.

d.  Can this function ever be equal to zero? Explain why or why not.

e.  Mr. Samuels bought his house in New York City in 1970. If the trend continued, how much was he likely to have paid? Explain and provide mathematical evidence to support your answer.

3. Veronica's physics class is analyzing the speed of a dropped object just before it hits the ground when it's dropped from different heights. They are comparing the final velocity, in feet/second, versus the height, in feet, from which the object was dropped. The class comes up with the following graph.

a. Use transformations of the parent function, $f(x) = \sqrt{x}$, to write an algebraic equation that represents this graph. Describe the domain in terms of the context.

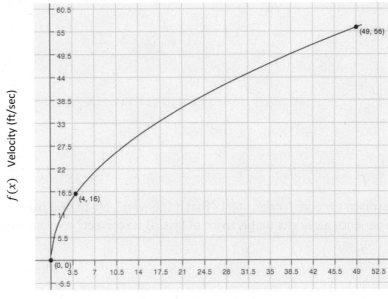

b.  Veronica and her friends are planning to go cliff diving at the end of the school year.  If she dives from a position that is 165 ft. above the water, at what velocity will her body be moving right before she enters the water?  Show your work and explain the level of precision you chose for your answer.

c.  Veronica's friend, Patrick, thinks that if she were able to dive from a 330-ft. position, she would experience a velocity that is twice as fast.  Is he correct?  Explain why or why not.

4. Suppose that Peculiar Purples and Outrageous Oranges are two different and unusual types of bacteria. Both types multiply through a mechanism in which each single bacterial cell splits into four. However, they split at different rates: Peculiar Purples split every 12 minutes, while Outrageous Oranges split every 10 minutes.

   a. If the multiplication rate remains constant throughout the hour and we start with three bacterial cells of each, after one hour, how many bacterial cells will there be of each type? Show your work and explain your answer.

   b. If the multiplication rate remains constant for two hours, which type of bacteria is more abundant? What is the difference between the numbers of the two bacterial types after two hours?

   c. Write a function to model the growth of Peculiar Purples and explain what the variable and parameters represent in the context.

d.  Use your model from part (c) to determine how many Peculiar Purples there will be after three splits, i.e., at time 36 minutes.  Do you believe your model has made an accurate prediction?  Why or why not?

e.  Write an expression to represent a different type of bacterial growth with an unknown initial quantity but in which each cell splits into 2 at each interval of time.

5. In a study of the activities of dolphins, a marine biologist made a slow-motion video of a dolphin swimming and jumping in the ocean with a specially equipped camera that recorded the dolphin's position with respect to the slow-motion time in seconds. Below is a piecewise quadratic graph, made from the slow-motion dolphin video, which represents a dolphin's vertical height (in feet, from the surface of the water) while swimming and jumping in the ocean, with respect to the slow-motion time (in seconds). Use the graph to answer the questions. [Note: The numbers in this graph are not necessarily real numbers from an actual dolphin in the ocean.]

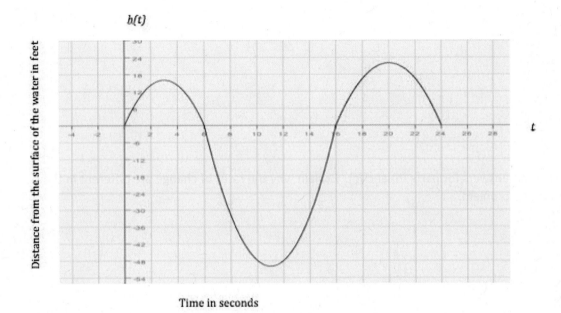

a. Given the vertex $(11, -50)$, write a function to represent the piece of the graph where the dolphin is underwater. Identify your variables and define the domain and range for your function.

b. Calculate the average rate of change for the interval from 6 to 8 seconds. Show your work and explain what your answer means in the context of this problem.

c.   Calculate the average rate of change for the interval from 14 to 16 seconds.  Show your work and explain what your answer means in the context of this problem.

d.   Compare your answers for parts (b) and (c).  Explain why the rates of change are different in the context of the problem.

6.  The tables below represent values for two functions, *f* and *g*, one absolute value and one quadratic.

a.  Label each function as either <u>absolute value</u> or <u>quadratic</u>.  Then explain mathematically how you identified each type of function.

*f*(*x*): _____

| $x$ | $f(x)$ |
|-----|--------|
| − 3 | 1.5 |
| − 2 | 1 |
| − 1 | 0.5 |
| 0 | 0 |
| 1 | 0.5 |
| 2 | 1 |
| 3 | 1.5 |

*g*(*x*): _____

| $x$ | $g(x)$ |
|-----|--------|
| − 3 | 4.5 |
| − 2 | 2 |
| − 1 | 0.5 |
| 0 | 0 |
| 1 | 0.5 |
| 2 | 2 |
| 3 | 4.5 |

b.  Represent each function graphically.  Identify and label the key features of each in your graph (e.g., vertex, intercepts, axis of symmetry, etc.).

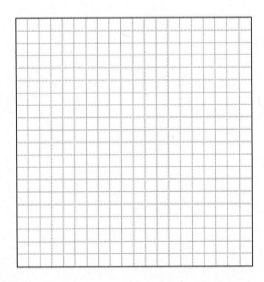

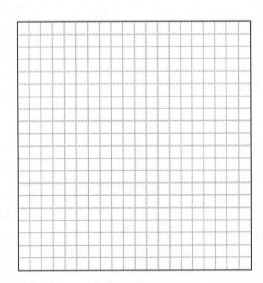

c.  Represent each function algebraically.

7. Wendy won a one million dollar lottery! She will receive her winnings over the course of 10 years, which means she will get a check for $100,000 each year. In her college economics class, she learned about inflation, a general percentage increase in prices and fall in the purchasing power of money over time. (This is why prices from the past are sometimes referred to as "adjusted for inflation.") The inflation rate varies; from 2003 to 2013 the average rate has been 2.36% per year. This means that the value of a fixed dollar amount has decreased by 2.36%, on average, per year.

a. Wendy wants to make sure she gets the most out of her winnings, so she wants to figure out how much purchasing power she will lose over the course of the 10 years. Assume the average inflation rate will remain the same for the next 10 years. Complete the table below to help her calculate her losses in purchasing power due to inflation.

| Year | Check Amount | Purchasing Power After Adjusted for Inflation | Loss in Purchasing Power |
|------|--------------|-----------------------------------------------|--------------------------|
| 0 | 100,000.00 | 100,000.00 | 0.00 |
| 1 | 100,000.00 | 97,640.00 | 2,360.00 |
| 2 | 100,000.00 | | |
| 3 | 100,000.00 | | |
| 4 | 100,000.00 | | |
| 5 | 100,000.00 | | |
| 6 | 100,000.00 | | |
| 7 | 100,000.00 | | |
| 8 | 100,000.00 | | |
| 9 | 100,000.00 | | |
| 10 | 100,000.00 | | |

b. The far right column shows the estimated loss in purchasing power for each year based on 2.36% inflation. Wendy would like to know what her total loss in purchasing power will likely be. Taking into account that inflation varies each year and 2.36% represents the average inflation rate over a period of years, report an answer to Wendy. What will her total estimated loss be? Choose an appropriate level of accuracy and show or explain how you got your answer.

**COMMON CORE**™   Module 5:   A Synthesis of Modeling with Equations and Functions
Date:   10/4/13

c.    James wrote the following equation to model this context: $P(t) = -2123.06t + 99612.56$. Tiah wrote the equation: $Q(t) = 100{,}000(0.9764^t)$. Which is a better model? Explain why.

d.    Wendy decides to try to offset the effects of inflation by investing $50,000, from her first check only, in a mutual fund with an annual 5% return. If she lets this money grow (i.e., she makes no deposits or withdrawals) for 10 years, will she make up the loss in purchasing power over the full 10 years?